Ancient Philosophers

Other Books in the History Makers series:

Ancient
Philosophers

By Don Nardo

LUCENT
BOOKS®

San Diego • Detroit • New York • San Francisco • Cleveland
New Haven, Conn. • Waterville, Maine • London • Munich

© 2004 by Lucent Books. Lucent Books is an imprint of The Gale Group, Inc.,
a division of Thomson Learning, Inc.

Lucent Books® and Thomson Learning™ are trademarks used herein under license.

For more information, contact
Lucent Books
27500 Drake Rd.
Farmington Hills, MI 48331-3535
Or you can visit our Internet site at http://www.gale.com

LIBRARY OF CONGRESS CATALOGING-IN-PUBLICATION DATA

Nardo, Don, 1947–.
    Ancient philosophers / by Don Nardo.
p. cm. — (History Makers)
Summary: Investigates the roots of philosophy, when it was still blended with science,
and profiles five philosophers from the distant past, considering how their thinking
contributed to society and civilizations.
Includes bibliographical references and index.
    ISBN 1-59018-281-2 (alk. paper)
    1. Philosophers, Ancient—Biography—Juvenile literature. [1. Philosophers.
2. Philosophy.] I. Title. II. I. Title. II. Series.
    B168.N37 S447 2004
    180—dc21

                                                                    200311234

Printed in the United States of America

Contents

The literary form most often referred to as "multiple biography" was perfected in the first century A.D. by Plutarch, a perceptive and talented moralist and historian who hailed from the small town of Chaeronea in central Greece. His most famous work, *Parallel Lives*, consists of a long series of biographies of noteworthy ancient Greek and Roman statesmen and military leaders. Frequently, Plutarch compares a famous Greek to a famous Roman, pointing out similarities in personality and achievements. These expertly constructed and very readable tracts provided later historians and others, including playwrights like Shakespeare, with priceless information about prominent ancient personages and also inspired new generations of writers to tackle the multiple biography genre.

The Lucent History Makers series proudly carries on the venerable tradition handed down from Plutarch. Each volume in the series consists of a set of five to eight biographies of important and influential historical figures who are linked together by a common factor. In *Rulers of Ancient Rome*, for example, all the figures were generals, consuls, or emperors of either the Roman Republic or Empire; while the subjects of *Fighters Against American Slavery*, though they lived in different places and times, all shared the same goal, namely the eradication of human servitude. Mindful that politicians and military leaders are not (and never have been) the only people who shape the course of history, the editors of the series have also included representatives from a wide range of endeavors, including scientists, artists, writers, philosophers, religious leaders, and sports figures.

Each book is intended to give a range of figures—some well known, others less known; some who made a great impact on history, others who made only a small impact. For instance, by making Columbus's initial voyage possible, Spain's Queen Isabella I, featured in *Women Leaders of Nations*, helped to open up the New World to exploration and exploitation by the European powers. Unarguably, therefore, she made a major contribution to a series of events that had momentous consequences for the entire world. By contrast, Catherine II, the eighteenth-century Russian queen, and Golda Meir, the modern Israeli prime minister, did not play roles of global impact; however, their policies and actions significantly influenced the historical development of both their own countries and their regional neighbors. Regardless of their relative importance in the greater historical scheme, all of the figures chronicled in the History Makers series made contributions to posterity; and their public achievements, as well as what is known about their private lives, are presented and evaluated in light of the most recent scholarship.

In addition, each volume in the series is documented and substantiated by a wide array of primary and secondary source quotations. The primary source quotes enliven the text by presenting eyewitness views of the times and culture in which each history maker lived; while the secondary source quotes, taken from the works of respected modern scholars, offer expert elaboration and/or critical commentary. Each quote is footnoted, demonstrating to the reader exactly where biographers find their information. The footnotes also provide the reader with the means of conducting additional research. Finally, to further guide and illuminate readers, each volume in the series features photographs, two bibliographies, and a comprehensive index.

The History Makers series provides both students engaged in research and more casual readers with informative, enlightening, and entertaining overviews of individuals from a variety of circumstances, professions, and backgrounds. No doubt all of them, whether loved or hated, benevolent or cruel, constructive or destructive, will remain endlessly fascinating to each new generation seeking to identify the forces that shaped their world.

Men Who Asked, "What, Why, and How?"

Today people are used to and comfortable with asking questions for which they can expect to receive definite answers. One might ask, for example, who won yesterday's baseball game and by how many runs. Or a person might want to know how many planets there are in our solar system. On hearing that the Boston Red Sox won by a score of 3 to 2 and that the solar system contains nine planets, the questioner feels a certain satisfaction; he or she asked a simple question and got a simple answer, with no loose ends and no need to expend any more energy thinking about it. Life is full of such simple questions and answers.

Now and then, however, the questions may seem simple, but the answers are far from it. How many baseball fans, for instance, would feel either comfortable or competent trying to answer questions such as: Why do people like to play? or is playing essential to living a good life? Similarly, who is qualified to answer the query: Did the matter that makes up the planets and solar system come into being by natural means or by divine intervention?

For the present, neither science nor religion can answer such questions with any surety. So they fall under the discipline of philosophy, which examines ideas and the meaning of life rather than proven facts. The term "philosophy" comes from an ancient Greek word meaning "love of wisdom." And philosophers certainly seek wisdom as they try to explain concepts with no definite answers. These concepts lie in a gray area, a sort of "No Man's Land between theology and science," as the great modern thinker Bertrand Russell puts it. Typical questions considered by philosophers through the ages, Russell says, include the following:

Is the world divided into mind and matter, and, if so, what is mind and what is matter? Is mind subject to matter, or is it possessed of independent powers? Has the universe any unity or purpose? . . . Are there really laws of nature, or do we believe in them only because of our innate love of order? . . . Is there a way of living that is noble and another that is base, or are all ways of living merely futile? . . . Is there such a thing as wisdom, or is what seems such merely the ultimate refinement of folly? To such questions, no answer can be found in the laboratory. . . . The studying of these questions, if not the answering of them, is the business of philosophy.[1]

This "business of philosophy" has been going on for a long time. Every modern philosopher has felt the influence of the ideas of his or her predecessors, and each of those predecessors was inspired or influenced by still older thinkers. Delving back far enough, one reaches the first important philosophers known to history. (There may well have been still earlier ones, but if so, they left no traces in the historical record.)

These ancient philosophers, like their modern counterparts, looked upon their world and asked what made it tick. What was its shape, of what substances was it composed, and what position did it occupy in the universe, or greater scheme of things? They

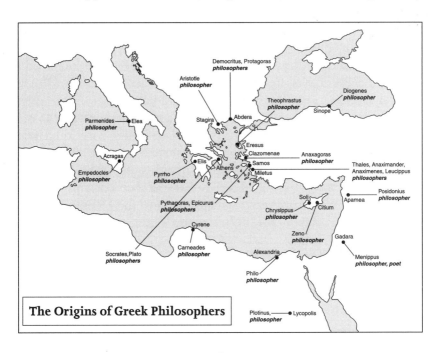

The Origins of Greek Philosophers

9

also wanted to know why the world existed. Who or what made Earth, and nature itself, in the first place and for what purpose? Moreover, how did human beings fit into the picture? How did people come to be? What is their purpose and their destiny, if any? And how should they live their lives?

Thinkers in the West

Among the first individuals who tried to answer such questions in Western (European-based) society was a Greek named Democritus, who lived in the fifth century B.C. He and another Greek named Leucippus were the first thinkers to propose that all substances in nature are composed of tiny, invisible particles. He called them by the name that they still bear—atoms. The atoms combine in numerous different ways, he said, which accounts for the vast number and diverse nature of the physical objects that exist. Democritus also related the atomic theory directly to the issue of how people should live their lives. Knowing the physical workings of nature brings people peace of mind, he said, and that peace of mind is the basis of happiness. To be happy, therefore, people should strive always to learn how nature works.

Most later Greek philosophers either rejected Democritus's ideas about atoms or ignored them. One of the most influential of all, a fourth-century B.C. Athenian named Plato, was less concerned with the exact makeup of matter and more with the moral and ethical behavior of human beings. People should strive to know what is good and just, he advocated. Once a person has discovered these truths, he or she is bound to act in a virtuous manner; by contrast, ignorance results in bad behavior.

Plato's pupil, Aristotle, is perhaps the most famous of all early Western philosophers. Aristotle was also deeply concerned with the nature of virtue, ethics, and moral behavior. In addition, he was preoccupied with a wide range of other questions about humans and nature that inspired his researches on and writings about politics, ideal governments, Earth and the planets, and animals and how they might be classified.

Thinkers in the East

While the early Western philosophers considered the major questions of nature and life, far to the east Chinese and Indian thinkers wrestled with these same concepts. In China, Confucius, a near contemporary of Democritus, was as concerned about politics as

This medieval painting attempts to depict some of the leading thinkers of the ancient Western world, including the Greeks Pythagoras, Aristotle, and Ptolemy, and the Roman Cicero.

A woman prays before a statue of the Buddha. Buddhism began in India and later spread to China, Korea, and other lands.

Aristotle was. Confucius felt that political disorder and bad government could be remedied by the good behavior of individuals. And such good behavior should be based on simple social norms, such as loyalty and personal responsibility, that had been prevalent in prior generations.

In India, too, deep thinkers were interested in the human condition, including both its negative and positive elements and how the negative ones might be alleviated. In the sixth century B.C., for instance, a nobleman named Siddhārtha set out to find the causes of suffering. He meditated, and suddenly these causes, as well as how they might be avoided, became apparent to him. Thereafter, he was known as the Buddha, or "Enlightened One." By following eight steps, including attaining understanding and speaking and acting properly, Buddha advocated, one can avoid suffering.

Effects of the Philosophers on Ordinary People

The importance of these ancient thinkers to ordinary people in later generations cannot be overstated. Buddha's philosophy of life was one of the most important in history, for example, partly because it became the basis for a new religion; moreover, Buddhism spread beyond India to China, Korea, Mongolia, Japan, Tibet, and elsewhere and today remains one of the predominant Asian faiths. Similarly, Confucius's teachings became part of the religious experience of billions of Chinese. Meanwhile, in the West, the ideas of Democritus, Plato, and Aristotle exerted a strong influence over medieval and modern thinkers (although none of their philosophies became part of a religion). Much of modern scientific thought was either built on or was a reaction to their ideas.

Thus, these thinkers were not simply odd characters dwelling in ivory towers remote from everyday experience, as depicted in a common stereotype of philosophers. They may have been eccentric, either socially or intellectually, in their own times. But their steadfast queries into the "what, why, and how" of existence came to affect the way millions of average people view the world and live their lives. In this way, they demonstrated how the discipline of philosophy affects ordinary people in all ages. In the words of John K. Roth, a professor of philosophy at California's Claremont McKenna College,

> Philosophy reflects and shows how questions and questionings are vital to our lives. Everything in life hinges on whether any person can rightly claim to possess knowledge. Hardly an hour passes without questions being raised as to whether we ought to do some things and not others. These issues keep us thinking about the future. Questions about the meaning and destiny of our lives—individually and collectively—are never far from our attention.[2]

CHAPTER 1

The Development of Ancient Philosophy

The history of ancient philosophy is filled with brilliant and insightful thinkers who advanced human knowledge or developed and expanded the intellectual process by which people obtain knowledge. The early philosophers also focused people's attention on abstract ideas about the universe and the human experience. These included the nature and purpose of the physical realm and existence within it and the meaning of concepts such as goodness, evil, truth, the soul, suffering, happiness, wisdom, community, duty, and justice.

In the West, comprising the lands making up what came to be called Europe (and the global societies it later spawned), these philosophical endeavors began in Greece. The ideas of Thales, Democritus, Anaxagoras, Socrates, Plato, Aristotle, and others were absorbed and sometimes developed by Roman thinkers. And in their turn, the Romans passed them along to medieval and early modern society, creating much of the Western intellectual tradition, including the rise of science in modern times.

The East, encompassing India, China, and other Asian lands, also produced a rich philosophical tradition. Thinkers such as Buddha, Confucius, Mencius, Lao-tzu, Chuang-tzu, and others also probed the nature of existence and humanity's place within it. Yet, for a long time, these men and the schools of thought they represented did not have a word corresponding to the Western term "philosophy." Instead, they saw themselves and their ideas as part of a larger theological, or religious, tradition. This is why ancient Western philosophy often led to materialistic intellectual disciplines, especially science, while ancient Eastern philosophy became incorporated into more mystical, religious realms of thought. As British scholar E.W.F. Tomlin puts it,

In the history of Western thought, there is a thing called philosophy and there is a thing called theology. And it has usually been possible . . . to distinguish between the two. In the history of Eastern thought, there is only a thing called theology. . . . Philosophy pursued as a secular [non-religious] game, a technique to be acquired at a university . . . to enable the student to be formidable in argument, is . . . a Western product. . . . In the [East] it is impossible to be a philosopher without being also a [religious] sage.[3]

The strong religious overtones of Eastern philosophy are perhaps the most obvious factor distinguishing it from its Western counterpart. There are other differences as well. However, the Western and Eastern branches of philosophy also have similarities; this was particularly true in their early years. Putting all other ideas and questions aside, virtually all ancient philosophers were concerned with the true meaning of life and the best, most positive ways for people to behave. This is only natural, since these thinkers were human first and either Westerners or Easterners second. "Those elements common to both Eastern and Western thought," Tomlin says, "should confirm us in the belief . . . that the human

The Greco-Roman gods dine in this Renaissance painting. Western philosophers believed the gods were subject to the same natural laws as people.

mind is everywhere one in the same, or at least that it operates in the same way."[4]

Philosophers or Scientists?

As for the ancient Greek mind, which produced the first great Western thinkers, much of it was shaped by the tendency to separate the material world from the spiritual, mystical world. At the time, this approach to knowledge was unprecedented in human history. Before the rise of the first important Greek thinkers in the sixth century B.C., all peoples everywhere accepted the idea that nature and human existence were the results of the will and whims of gods or other divine or superhuman beings. The Greek philosophers, in contrast, largely removed the gods and other supernatural elements from their inquiries into the nature of existence.

Most of these philosophers accepted the existence of the gods. And they did not doubt that these powerful beings could punish, reward, and otherwise interact with humans. Yet as modern scientists do, the Greek thinkers viewed the universe as an organized system that operated by natural, quite impersonal laws—what they called a cosmos. In their view, the gods were simply superhuman entities who shared that cosmos with humans and were as subject to its natural laws as people were. This tremendous intellectual breakthrough made possible the entire later development of Western philosophy and science. In awe of the early Greek thinkers, the first-century B.C. Roman scholar Lucretius remarked,

A bust of Socrates, who was primarily concerned with the moral aspects of philosophy.

> When human life lay groveling . . . under the dead weight of superstition . . . a man from Greece was first to raise mortal eyes in

defiance. . . . Fables and the gods did not crush him, nor the lightning flash and the growling menace of the sky. Rather . . . he, first of all men, longed to smash the constraining locks of nature's doors. The vital vigor of his mind prevailed. He ventured far out beyond the flaming ramparts of the world and voyaged in mind throughout infinity. . . . Superstition, in its turn, lies crushed beneath his feet, and we, by his triumph, are lifted level with the skies.[5]

From a modern viewpoint, Lucretius was both a philosopher and a scientist. In this respect, he had much in common with the men who made up the first few generations of Greek truthseekers, who lived and worked in the sixth and fifth centuries B.C. (They are often called the pre-Socratics because they preceded the major Athenian philosopher Socrates, whose ideas directly and profoundly influenced Plato, Aristotle, and other later intellectual giants.) In fact, during this early period, there was as yet no clear distinction between science and philosophy. Today philosophy is a field of endeavor in which one begins by observing a phenomenon and then speculates about the causes and meaning of it without the need to back up the argument with tangible proof. By contrast, a scientist observes a phenomenon and then collects data and performs experiments in an attempt to discover and prove its cause or causes. Most ancient Greek thinkers, especially the pre-Socratics, mixed these two approaches in varying degrees. According to University of Geneva scholar Jonathan Barnes,

> We should regard the Presocratics as the first investigators of matters which became the special objects of astronomy, physics, chemistry, zoology, botany, physiology, and so on. At the other end of the scale, the Presocratic enterprise involved much larger and more obviously "philosophical" questions: did the universe have a beginning? And if so, how did it begin? What are its basic constituents? . . . What can we hope to learn about it? Not all the Presocratics asked all these questions. . . . But they all [thought and] wrote within that general framework. . . . Whether we should now call them philosophers or scientists or both is a matter of no importance.[6]

The Ionian Philosophers

Most of the Greek pre-Socratics belonged to a few general schools of thought or intellectual traditions. One of these grew in the

Greek city-states situated on the western coast of Asia Minor (what is now Turkey). In ancient times this region was known as Ionia, so these men belonged to what came to be called the Ionian tradition. The first major Ionian thinker was Thales, who was born in the prosperous city of Miletus sometime before 600 B.C. In his quest to understand the cosmos and explain its workings in simple, rational terms, he tried to define a single physical principle that he assumed must underlie the whole system. He called this principle the *physis* (from which the term "physics" derives). Thales left no writings. But fortunately, some later Greek thinkers discussed his views, including Aristotle, who wrote that Thales

> declared the *physis* to be water, and for that reason he also held that the earth rests upon water. Probably the idea was suggested to him by the fact that the nutriment of everything contains moisture, and that heat itself is generated out of moisture and is kept alive by it. . . . He drew his notion also from the fact that the seeds of everything have a moist nature. . . . The earth stays in place, he explained, because it floats like wood or some such substance of nature to let it float upon water but not upon air.[7]

This theory of a wet universe proved to be incorrect, of course. Yet Thales was important because he inspired his pupils and other later Greek thinkers to search for material, rather than supernatural, explanations of nature and its workings. One of the first to take up this challenge was Thales' student, Anaximander, who flourished in the mid-sixth century B.C. Anaximander disagreed with the notion that water was the underlying principle of nature. Instead, he said, the cosmos and everything in it are composed of an eternal, unchanging, and invisible substance that he called the "Boundless." From the Boundless, Anaximander postulated, arose the four major natural elements—earth, water, air, and fire.

Anaximander also proposed a theory for the origins of life. The first living creatures arose in water, he said. Later they crawled onto the dry land and adapted themselves to their new surroundings, becoming various species, including humans. "Man came into being from an animal other than himself," Anaximander is credited with writing, "namely the fish, which in early times he resembled."[8] (This theory of organic evolution was extraordinarily similar to the one developed in the nineteenth century by English biologist Charles Darwin.)

Another Ionian thinker, Anaximander's pupil Anaximenes, accepted his mentor's idea about the origins of living things. However, in his quest to understand the nature of the *physis*, Anaximenes rejected both water and the Boundless. He proposed instead that nature's underlying principal is air. By thinning out, he said, air sometimes turns into fire, and by becoming denser (more compact), air becomes water and water becomes earth.

The last of the major Ionian thinkers, was Anaximenes' student Anaxagoras. In contrast with his predecessors, Anaxagoras did not single out one element as nature's primary substance. He suggested

The first Ionian Greek philosopher-scientist, Thales, proposed that water is the major underlying principle of nature.

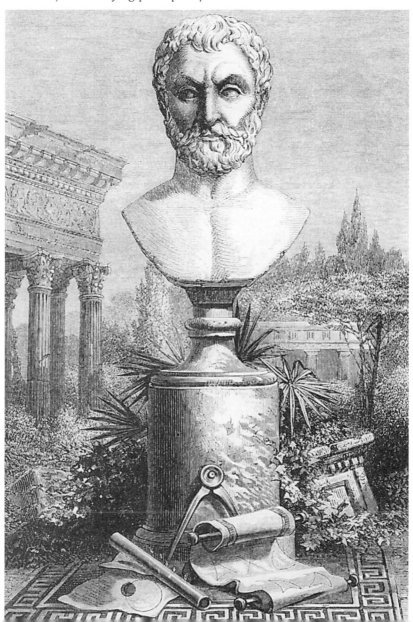

instead that manifestations of all of the substances in nature are present in all things. This supposition grew partly from his observations of the act of eating and its consequences. After people eat bread, fruits, and vegetables, Anaxagoras pointed out, they grow flesh, bones, skin, and hair. In his view, this occurs because the "seeds" of flesh, bones, skin, and

Another Ionian, Anaxagoras, held that the seeds of nature's basic substances exist in all things.

hair exist in the food when it is eaten. How else "could hair come from what is not hair, or flesh from what is not flesh?" he asked. Thus, he concluded, the tiny seeds of all things must have existed from the beginning of time and "in everything there is a little bit of everything else."[9]

Later Greek and Roman Thinkers

Another major group of early Greek thinkers lived in the Greek cities that sprang up in southern Italy in the seventh century B.C. One of these cities, Crotona, produced Pythagoras, whose followers studied mathematics, astronomy, music, theology, and other subjects. A number of the Pythagoreans suggested that numbers constitute the *physis*, nature's underlying principle. "It seemed to the Pythagoreans," Aristotle later wrote, "that they could discover in numbers, more truly than in fire or earth or water" an explanation of nature's structure.

> For instance, they explained justice as a certain property of number, soul and mind as another such . . . and they gave the same kind of [numerical] interpretation to virtually everything else as well. . . . Since they found . . . that every-

thing . . . seemed to be essentially numerical . . . they concluded that the elements of numbers must be the elements of everything, and that the visible heavens in their entirety consist of harmony and number.[10]

Part of this heavenly harmony, said the Pythagorean thinkers, was a variety of spheres nesting within one another; one sphere held Earth, another held the stars and planets, and a third, more distant one served as the realm of the gods. Core elements of this scheme influenced later Greek thinkers, including Aristotle himself.

Still another group of Greek thinkers are today often called the atomists because their philosophical ideas revolved around the notion that nature is made up of tiny separate particles. Leucippus, who lived in the fifth century B.C., and Democritus, his younger contemporary, were early champions of atomism. A later Greek thinker, Epicurus, developed and promoted their ideas, as did the Roman philosopher Lucretius.

Thus, interest in nature's workings, which had largely preoccupied the pre-Socratics, continued among Western thinkers even after Socrates came on the scene in the late fifth century B.C. (Aristotle was especially interested in the natural sciences, for example.) However, Socrates emphasized another aspect of philosophy that thereafter became central to the discipline. Namely, he sought to

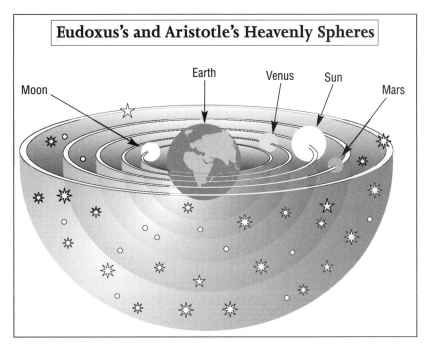

Eudoxus's and Aristotle's Heavenly Spheres

understand what goodness is and whether or not it could be taught. Socrates believed that knowledge of goodness could lead to correct behavior, which in turn could lead to happiness. Plato and Aristotle also expended considerable time and energy exploring the concept of goodness and how people might attain it and thereby improve society.

The direction of Western philosophical endeavor took another turn after Plato and Aristotle, however. Most later schools of thought, including the Greek Epicureans and Roman Stoics, seemed to resign themselves to the idea that they could *not* improve society. So they directed their energies to teaching people to be as happy as possible in a largely miserable, unpredictable, and unchangeable world.

Indian Traditions: Suffering and the Self

Meanwhile, in faraway India, deep thinkers did not resign themselves to accepting the imperfect world and adjusting their philosophy to accommodate inevitable misery and injustice.

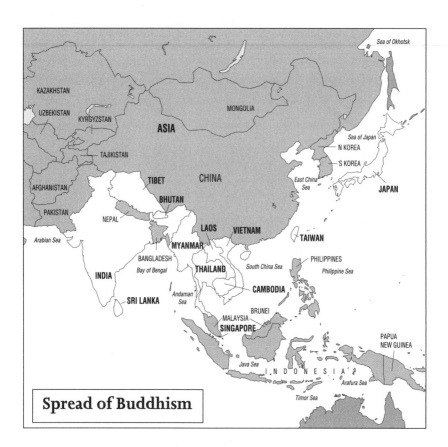

Spread of Buddhism

Early Indian philosophy was practical in character, like that of Socrates and Plato. "From the very beginning," explains scholar John M. Koller,

> the speculation of India's sages was aimed at solving life's basic problems. Their philosophy grew out of their attempts to improve life. Confronted with physical, mental, and spiritual suffering, India's early sages sought to understand the reasons and causes for this suffering. They attempted to improve their understanding of [humanity] and the universe because they wanted to uproot the causes of suffering and to achieve the best possible life.[11]

The varying solutions proposed by these early thinkers developed into several related yet distinctive schools of thought. The most influential of these groups was Sāmkhya, probably founded in the sixth or fifth century B.C. by a thinker named Kapila. Sāmkhya doctrine recognizes and differentiates between two eternal, underlying principles. The first, *prakriti*, is nature's material principle or structure (roughly corresponding to the Greek *physis*). Separate from material concerns is the other underlying principle—*purusha*, usually defined as pure consciousness.

Indian philosophy teaches that most humans traditionally fall for the illusion that *prakriti* and *purusha* (in a sense matter and soul, or nonself and self) are the same or at least inseparable. This ignorance leads to suffering. And the only way to end suffering is to seek, find, and appreciate the self, separate from the nonself. Another Indian school of thought, Yoga, whose most famous early advocate was a thinker named Patañjali, was devoted to this goal. To alleviate ignorance, followers of Yoga advocated physical and mental discipline, including deep meditation.

Another originally Indian school of thought, Buddhism, was strongly influenced by these concepts. According to tradition, the founder of the movement, Buddha, recognized the existence of suffering and discovered a way to avoid it. "I teach only two things," he is credited with saying, "the fact of suffering and the possibility of escape from suffering."[12] Buddha worked out a systematic series of steps intended to help a person achieve selflessness and a release from ignorance and suffering.

Early Chinese Philosophy

Buddhism eventually made its way to China, where it became very popular. But it did not supplant the native philosophical-religious

This old engraving depicts the Chinese thinker Lao-tzu, founder of Taoism, a philosophy that rejects worldly ideas and actions.

systems that already existed there. The major ones included Confucianism, established by Confucius and later developed by Mencius and others, and Taoism, founded by Lao-tzu and later expanded on by Chuang-tzu and others.

While Confucius and Mencius stressed the importance of social and political traditions and institutions, the Taoist thinkers rejected these and other worldly ideas and actions. Lao-tzu and Chuang-tzu held that a very basic, invisible, but ever-present principle or force pervades all of nature. That principle is known as the *tao* (pronounced DOW). Humans, they said, should allow the *tao* to do its work, maintain order and rightness, and not involve themselves in politics. Thus, the Confucians sought an enlightened way of life through direct, honest, and constructive involvement in politics and other worldly institutions. In contrast, the Taoists searched for enlightenment in noninvolvement. They opted for avoiding traditional political and social activity so as to devote proper time and energy to contemplating their own place in the true harmony of nature. Confucianism was more practical, therefore, and Taoism more mystical.

Instead of competing with these philosophies, Buddhism complemented and even blended with them. "In the centuries following Buddhism's first appearance in China," writes scholar Nancy W. Ross,

> a vital exchange of ideas [took place] between this transplanted teaching and the two classic Chinese philosophies, Taoism and Confucianism. Together, in time, these three philosophies might be said to have created a fourth, a subtle blend of them all . . . Zen.[13]

In a sense, then, Zen Buddhism, which soon spread to Japan, tended to mix the worldly practicality of Confucianism with Taoism's mystical contemplation and Buddhism's meditation into the self. "The Zen 'awakening' is not supposed to bring withdrawal from the world," Ross points out. Rather, it encourages participation in worldly affairs, except for those that might bring strife or hurt someone else. The follower of Zen meditates, but in doing so "is not seeking something superhuman." He or she does not aspire to be a saint or totally enlightened being (as Buddha was said to be). "He simply wants to . . . discover his 'true self,'" and thereby to feel liberated and at peace.[14]

This strong emphasis on self-examination is reminiscent of that undertaken by the Greek thinker Socrates. The ancient Western and Eastern philosophical traditions had many differences. But the search for the underlying truth of human existence was a core tenet common to both.

CHAPTER 2

Democritus: What Is Nature's Underlying Structure?

One of the most important early Western thinkers, Democritus, is remembered primarily for his development of the atomic theory. Yet this accomplishment was only one of many in a long and productive career. In fact, Democritus was one of the most versatile of the Greco-Roman philosophers, as reflected by the fact that his writings covered astronomy, mathematics, biology, medicine, geography, anthropology, psychology, ethics, and more. According to the third-century A.D. Greek biographer Diogenes Laertius, who wrote a short sketch of Democritus's life,

> Truly, Democritus was versed in every department of philosophy, for he had trained himself both in physics and in ethics, nay more, in mathematics and the routine subjects of education, and he was quite an expert in the arts.[15]

Diogenes further asserted that, out of jealousy for Democritus's incredible versatility and expansive knowledge, the renowned Athenian philosopher Plato wanted to burn all of his predecessor's works. "Plato, who mentions almost all the early philosophers, never once alludes to Democritus," said Diogenes, "obviously because he knew that he would have to match himself against the prince of philosophers."[16] This charge against Plato is almost certainly false. But the fact that it and similar tall tales about scholarly jealousy circulated in ancient times shows how widely Democritus was respected.

Democritus's considerable reputation in the ancient world was based on his many writings. Indeed, the enormous breadth of his interests and expertise can be seen in the sheer number and diversity of the titles of these works. Only a few of those listed by Diogenes include *Description of the World, On the Planets, Causes of*

Celestial Phenomena, On Nature, On Geography, On Geometry, On Reason, On the Senses, On Tranquility, On Virtue, On the Soul, On the Criteria of Logic, On Poetry, On Diet, and *On Fighting in Armor*. Sadly, none of these or any of Democritus's other works has survived intact. Only a few fragments remain, along with some brief quotes from his writings or summaries of them in the works of later writers. Considering the brilliance of his ideas about atoms, the disappearance of Democritus's great body of work may well be one of the most tragic losses humanity has ever suffered.

Abdera's Native Son

Democritus was born in about 460 B.C. in Abdera, a small port town on the northern coast of the Aegean Sea. At the time, it was the most prosperous port in southern Thrace (the ancient name for the region lying north of the Aegean). In addition to shipping interests, the Abderites owned many large wheat fields and vineyards; this inspired them to stamp the image of an ear of grain on their coins.

Democritus, pictured here examining an animal, was one of the most versatile of the Greek thinkers.

On the negative side, Abdera had a reputation for being the home of backward, stupid people, which made it the butt of cruel jokes across the Greek world. Perhaps this stemmed from the fact that the town existed in an outlying area, far from major Greek economic and cultural centers such as Athens, Corinth, and Miletus. Also, the hinterlands of Thrace were populated largely by uneducated, uncultured tribal groups. But the charge that Abdera was an intellectual backwash was unfounded. The town's native sons

A medieval woodcut depicts one of the more important ancient Greek thinkers Anaxagoras.

included not only Democritus, one of the greatest thinkers of the ancient world, but also the noted philosopher Protagoras (best known for saying, "Man is the measure of all things") and other scholars.

As for Democritus's own boyhood education, little is known for sure. Diogenes said that he studied with some Persian scholars who lived in Abdera. (If so, they may have originally been part of the expedition of Persia's King Xerxes, who had invaded Greece by way of Thrace shortly before Democritus was born.) Also, Diogenes reported, the young Democritus met the noted Greek philosopher Anaxagoras, who "did not take to him."[17] This sounds like another later tall tale designed to magnify Democritus's reputation by suggesting that noted thinkers were jealous of his brilliance.

A Young World Traveler

Likely more reliable are ancient accounts that claim the young Democritus sought to expand his educational opportunities by traveling to cities and lands known for their scholarly endeavors. He went to Egypt to study geometry, for instance. From there, he headed northeastward into Persia, whose priest-scholars had access to the accumulated knowledge of the ancient Mesopotamian

Democritus contemplates the idea that all of the varied objects surrounding him are made up of atoms, particles too tiny for people to see.

peoples, including the Sumerians and Babylonians. Democritus may even have continued on to India, then an almost-legendary land on the outer fringe of the known world. "I am the most widely traveled man of all my contemporaries," he said in a surviving fragment, "and have pursued inquiries in the most distant places; I have visited more countries and climes [climates] than anyone else, and have listened to the teachings of more learned men."[18]

Democritus apparently paid for these trips by taking his share of the family inheritance in cash. Diogenes said that he was the youngest of three sons. And after his father's death, he "chose the smaller portion" of the inheritance, which was in the form of money rather than property, "because he had need of this to pay the cost of travel."[19]

At some point in his young manhood, Democritus used part of the money to fund a trip to Athens, then widely viewed as the leading cultural center of the Greek world. Exactly what he did and who he met there are unknown. In fact, the only surviving description of the visit by Democritus himself is this fragment: "I came to Athens and no one knew me."[20] Centuries later Diogenes interpreted this to mean that Democritus "was not anxious to be recognized because he despised fame."[21] Another ancient writer suggested that Democritus viewed the Athenians as beneath his dignity. Neither of these scenarios seems to fit his character, however. The truth is likely simpler— that no one knew him because he arrived in Athens before he had gained fame as a philosopher and writer.

The title page of a sixteenth-century edition of a book by Aristotle, who recorded Democritus's ideas for posterity.

Leucippus, the Full, and the Empty

One Greek thinker who was already well known when Democritus was young was Leucippus, probably a native of Miletus, on the western coast of Asia Minor (although the exact location of his birthplace remains uncertain). Diogenes said that Democritus met Leucippus. Whether this was the result of the older man visiting Abdera or the younger one traveling to Miletus is unknown. What is important is that the core ideas for Democritus's most famous thesis—the atomic theory—came from Leucippus. (Today it is impossible to tell how much of the theory came from each man; however, most scholars believe that Democritus contributed the most, as well as explained it in more detail.)

Like most other early Greek philosophers, Leucippus wanted to know the true nature of the material world, including the *physis*, the principle or substance of which all things are made. These other thinkers generally held that, whatever that substance was, it was continuous; that is, it occupied all of space without interruption. The Greeks called this continuous quality of matter a plenum. In Leucippus's view, the existence of a plenum did not make sense, for how could one continuous, unchanging substance produce the great diversity of natural substances and objects?

Instead, said Leucippus, and Democritus agreed with him, the main substance making up worldly matter has two basic properties. These are the "being" and the "non-being," or the "full" and the "empty," or the "solid" and the "void" (depending on the translation). The being, or the full, is the matter that people can see and touch, whereas the non-being, or the empty, is empty space, or the absence of matter, today called a vacuum. Aristotle later wrote:

> Leucippus and his colleague Democritus say that the full and the void are elements, calling the one "being" and the other "non-being"; and of these, the full and solid is being, the void non-being . . . and these are the material causes of the things that exist.[22]

The obvious implication of this view is that the full consists of individual units separated from one another by the spaces that make up the empty. Leucippus and Democritus called these solid units, or particles, atoms. They are infinite in number, they said, and much too small to be seen by the eye. Moreover, the atoms have many different shapes, sizes, and arrangements.

The huge multiplicity of objects and substances in nature is therefore the result of atoms of various sizes and shapes forming diverse and distinctive groups. In this view, material objects are created when atoms come together. Further, these objects alter their forms when the atoms regroup and cease to exist when the atoms disperse. And all the qualities of these objects that seem obvious—such as color, taste, or temperature—are simply manifestations of the way the atoms move and congregate. The famous second-century A.D. Greco-Roman physician Galen tried to explain Democritus's atomic theory this way:

> Men think that there are white things and black things and sweet things and bitter things; but in truth everything is things and nothing—that is just what Democritus said, calling the atoms "things" and the void "nothing." Now, all the atoms, being small bodies, lack qualities. The void is a sort of space in which all these bodies move up and down for the whole of time, and either entangle with one another or strike and rebound, and in these meetings they disassociate [come apart] and again associate [come together] with one another and from this they make all compounds, including our own bodies and their properties and perceptions.[23]

The Creation and the Soul

Democritus did not merely propose and describe atoms. He also applied his atomic theory to a wide range of intellectual disciplines. In cosmology (the study of the origins of universe), for example, he suggested that the creation of the heavenly bodies was a random process involving atoms. These particles moved haphazardly through the empty, he said. Sometimes they collided with one another, in which case the larger ones tended to cluster together. This continued until the heavier, "earthy" substances formed and gathered in the center of the universe. These clumps of material became Earth, the planets, and other solid heavenly bodies. While this was happening, Democritus said, the lighter atoms began to move in a circular motion around Earth and formed the lighter known elements, such as air and fire.

Perhaps even more controversial was the manner in which Democritus tied the atomic theory to the less tangible and emotional subject of the human soul and what happened to it after death. Like everything, else, he claimed, the soul is made up of atoms. But these atoms are of a special kind. Extremely light and subtle in their movements, they float through the air until they enter the bodies of humans and animals. There they long remain, thanks to the act of breathing in and out, which keeps these unusual particles from escaping. "In animals that breathe," Aristotle wrote, describing Democritus's theory of the soul, their breathing keeps the soul

> from being squeezed out from the body. . . . For in the air
> there are many such particles which he identifies with mind
> and soul. When we breathe and air enters, these enter along
> with it, and by withstanding the pressure they prevent the
> soul in the animal from being forced out. Democritus thus
> explains why life and death are bound up with respiration.
> Death occurs when the surrounding air [in the lungs]
> presses upon the soul to such a degree that the animal can
> no longer respire. . . . Death is the departure of [the atoms
> comprising the soul] because of pressures from the air that
> surrounds them. It occurs not haphazardly, but by reason
> either of old age, which is natural, or of violence, which is
> unnatural. But Democritus does not offer any clear expla-
> nation of why this process goes on and why all must die.[24]

Aristotle's point that Democritus's theory of atoms did not explain everything about death was well-taken. In fact, on a number of counts, Democritus's ideas were either incomplete or, as modern science has shown, just plain wrong. His Earth-centered cosmology was incorrect, for instance. And no evidence has yet been discovered to support his conception of a soul made up of "light" atoms trapped in the body by the pressures of breathing. Still, Democritus was right about the existence of atoms and the fact that they do combine in diverse ways to form the many elements and objects in nature. This realization, which would not be ultimately proven until modern times, was one of the supreme intellectual achievements of

The paths of the heavenly bodies around Earth, as envisioned by Democritus's critic, Aristotle.

33

A fanciful depiction of Democritus shows him studying geography. His actual physical attributes are unknown.

the ancient world. Democritus's atomic theory, Jonathan Barnes remarks, "may be regarded from a certain point of view as the culmination of early Greek thought."[25]

Democritus Settles Down

It is unclear when Democritus began thinking about atoms or how long it took him to work out the various aspects of his atomic theory. Probably he worked on it during his travels, which seem to have continued off and on until he was in his early or mid-forties (about 420–415 B.C.). At that point, he returned to his family home in Abdera. Diogenes and a few other ancient writers claimed that he had run out of money, having finally spent all of his inheritance. At this point, it seemed that Democritus was destined for a life of extreme poverty. Fortunately for him, however, his brother Damasus took pity on him and provided him with financial support.

Thus, Democritus was able to continue with his research and philosophical conjecture. And over the next several years, he turned out a large number of treatises covering a wide range of subjects. He wrote about politics, foreshadowing the later political writings of Plato and Aristotle; moreover, it appears that, unlike these later thinkers, Democritus favored democracy. "Poverty in a democracy," he wrote, "is preferable to what is called prosperity among tyrants—by as much as liberty is preferable to slavery." He also believed that a good and just government was one that looked after the weakest and least fortunate members of the community:

> When those in power take it upon themselves to lend to the poor and to aid them and to favor them, then is there pity and no isolation, but companionship and mutual defense, and concord among the citizens and other good things too many to catalogue.[26]

In addition, Democritus was fascinated by the conditions in which human beings had lived before they had advanced enough to form communities and political institutions. His vision of early groups of hunter-gatherers, summarized by a later Greek writer, Diodorus Siculus, is striking in its accuracy and foresight:

> The first men lived an . . . animal sort of life, going out to forage individually and living off the most palatable herbs and the fruit which grew wild on the trees. Then, since they were attacked by wild animals, they helped one another. . . . The sounds they made had no sense and were confused; but gradually they articulated their expressions, and by establishing symbols among themselves for every sort of object, they [developed language]. . . . Such groups came into existence throughout the inhabited world, and not all men had the same language. . . . Hence, [today] there are languages of every type. . . . Now, the earliest men lived laboriously. . . . They wore no clothes, they knew nothing of dwelling-places or of fire, and they had not the slightest conception of cultivated produce. . . . Later, gradually instructed by experience, they took refuge in caves during the winter and stored those fruits that

This thirteenth-centuy painting of a hunter with his kill captures Democritus's largely accurate depiction of early humans as hunter-gatherers.

could be preserved. Once fire and other utilities were recognized, the crafts and whatever else can benefit communal life were slowly discovered.[27]

An Unusually Long Life

In time, Democritus's writings brought him fame and money. According to Diogenes, most of the money came from his fellow citizens of Abdera, who listened to him give public readings of his works. After Democritus had read "the best of all his works," Diogenes wrote, they "rewarded [him] with 500 talents [a huge amount of money at the time] and, more than that, with bronze statues as well."[28]

The proud citizens of Abdera also awarded their world-famous native son with a public funeral following his death. Democritus died in about 360 B.C. at the age of one hundred. Such longevity was extremely unusual at the time, as average life expectancy was between thirty and forty. Diogenes gave this account of the great philosopher's last few days:

> His sister was vexed that he seemed likely to die during the [religious] festival of Thesmophoria and she would be prevented from paying the fitting worship to the goddess. He bade her be of good cheer and ordered hot [compresses] to be brought to him every day. By applying these to his nostrils, he contrived to outlive the festival; and as soon as the three festival days were passed, he let his life go from him without pain.[29]

It is impossible to know what Democritus was thinking in his last moments. He may have been wondering what lay ahead in the undiscovered country of death, or he may have been mentally reviewing the highlights of his long, productive life. What seems certain is that he thoroughly enjoyed life. According to ancient sources, he believed that people should be as cheerful as humanly possible and enjoy life's few pleasures. "A life without feasts is a long road without inns," he is credited with saying. In fact, Democritus came to be known as the "Laughing Philosopher." Whether or not this nickname was truly reflective of his personality, and regardless of how happy his life had been, he could at least look back on his long list of intellectual achievements. He is reported to have said, "I would rather discover a single causal explanation than become king of the Persians."[30] In fleshing out the first atomic theory, Democritus certainly accomplished that goal.

CHAPTER 3

Plato: What Is the Meaning of Justice?

The Athenian Plato was a younger contemporary of Democritus's. Perhaps ten or twelve years old when the older philosopher concluded his travels and settled down for good in faraway Abdera, Plato likely never met him. Yet it is certain that Plato was familiar with Democritus's ideas. After all, Plato's pupil, Aristotle, mentioned the great atomist numerous times in his own writings. Plato and Democritus addressed some of the same topics—the nature of visible matter, cosmology, politics, and the soul, to name just a few. Yet the younger thinker drew noticeably different conclusions than the older one. Another difference between the two men was that while none of Democritus's treatises survived intact to the present, *all* of Plato's did. In part, this was because Plato's ideas exerted a tremendous influence on later Greco-Roman and European scholars, and they were careful to copy and recopy his works for posterity.

Plato's great influence as a philosopher was based on two major achievements. The first was his preservation of the personality and ideas of his mentor, Socrates, one of the most profound thinkers of all times. A poor, eccentric social outcast, the older man left no writings of his own, and if it had not been for Plato and a few other young admirers (including the Athenian historian Xenophon), Socrates might have been forgotten.

Plato's second and even greater accomplishment was to formulate his own philosophy, much of which developed and expanded on Socrates' basic views. Like Socrates, Plato asked fundamental questions such as What is goodness? What is truth? What is justice? And the process by which Plato attempted to answer these questions became a model for later thinkers to follow. In a now-famous comment, the English philosopher Alfred North Whitehead called the entire Western philosophical tradition "a series of footnotes to Plato."[31] This is an exaggeration, to be sure. Yet it cannot be denied that all Western thinkers since Plato have either incorporated his ideas into their own worldview or felt the need to explain why they disagreed with him.

From Pride to Bitterness

Part of Plato's authority and effectiveness as a philosopher, Whitehead points out, came from "his wide opportunities for experience at a great period of civilization."[32] This refers to the fact that Plato was born in Athens during that city-state's cultural golden age, which roughly spanned the fifth century B.C. Just prior to 500 B.C., Athens established the world's first democracy, which became more liberal and open in the decades that followed. In 480 B.C. the city gained a heroic reputation for helping to lead the rest of Greece in a stunning victory over a huge invading army of Persians. Then a series of Athenian statesmen consolidated over a hundred Greek states into a prosperous empire controlled by Athens, which used its enormous newfound wealth to erect temples and other large-scale structures. Among these buildings was the Parthenon, centerpiece of a magnificent temple complex on the city's central hill, the Acropolis. Athens also produced legendary poets, playwrights, and painters in this period. And for a brief and shining historical moment, the Athenians could legitimately boast that their city was the most beautiful, enlightened, and powerful in the Mediterranean world.

Plato was a follower of Socrates and founder of the Academy.

Plato entered this unique historical-cultural picture in 427 B.C., shortly after the Parthenon was completed. His father, Ariston, and mother, Perictione, were well-to-do aristocrats, so they could afford to hire the best teachers to tutor him.

The Agora, or marketplace, at Athens, more or less as it appeared when Plato was an old man.

These men dutifully taught the boy not only reading, writing, mathematics, and the verses of the great Greek poet Homer, but also feelings of great pride in Athens's power and cultural splendor.

Yet the young Plato was also shaped by the political and social realities that he witnessed as he was growing up. Not long before his birth, Athens and its allies had gone to war against the city-state of Sparta and its own allies. This conflict, the Peloponnesian War, turned out to be long and devastating, and it cost the Athenians massive casualties and economic privations. In 404 B.C., when Plato was twenty-three, his city finally was defeated and temporarily suffered the loss of its cherished democracy. All of this killing and social and political upheaval made Plato increasingly angry and bitter.

The Influence of Socrates

Two other factors that heavily shaped young Plato's worldview were the teachings of the philosopher Socrates and the latter's cruel fate, which made the younger man even more bitter and disillusioned. The two probably met when Plato was a child. At the time, the Athenian Charmides, Plato's uncle, and another Athenian, Critias, the boy's second cousin, were already avid followers of

Socrates. Through these relatives, Plato became acquainted with Socrates, and by about 407 B.C. the young man had become a disciple, too.

Almost every Athenian knew who Socrates was—an impoverished little man who dressed plainly in a loincloth covered by an unadorned piece of cloth wrapped in folds around his body. He was short and chubby, had a snubbed nose with wide, flaring nostrils, and seemed almost to waddle like a duck when he walked. Yet his ignoble physical features were deceiving to say the least. Socrates' intellect was keen and penetrating, and his personality was witty, compelling, and so brutally honest that some people found him disturbing.

A self-described social critic, Socrates wandered through the city and whenever possible chatted or argued with fellow citizens. Almost always, he urged them to take stock of themselves and to seek after justice and truth. The method he used in these encounters was to ask a series of penetrating questions about a subject. He would profess that he did not know the answers, although he often did. Meanwhile, the answers the person gave became a sort of trail leading to the discovery of the truth of that subject, at least as it related to him or her. This approach to inquiry and learning eventually became known as the "Socratic method" in Socrates' honor. Plato learned firsthand that a session with Socrates was bound to be enlightening but could also be challenging and even unnerving. In a work titled *Laches*, Plato later wrote:

Socrates wanders through the Athenian streets, ready to engage any and all in conversation.

41

Anyone who has an intellectual affinity to Socrates and enters into conversation with him is liable to be drawn into an argument; and whatever subject he may start, he will be continually carried round and round by him, until at last he finds that he has to give an account both of his present and past life; and when he is once entangled, Socrates will not let him go until he has completely and thoroughly sifted him.[33]

From Socrates, Plato learned the value of questioning everything about one's self and one's society, including the authority and actions of those who governed that society. Plato also learned about the true meaning of justice and courage from the events of Socrates' darkest, though finest hour. In 399 B.C., the Athenian government accused the old philosopher of corrupting the city's youth and then prosecuted, tried, and executed him. The charge was completely trumped up. And Plato was deeply angry and disheartened by what he viewed as a great injustice. "This was the end of our friend," he later wrote, "concerning

French artist Jacques-Louis David's magnificent painting of Socrates bidding his friends farewell before drinking poison.

whom I may truly say, that of all the men . . . I have known, he was the wisest and most just and best."[34]

A Noble Goal

The trial and execution of Socrates marked an important turning point in Plato's life. At the age of twenty-eight, the younger man no longer felt comfortable in his native city nor compelled to enter government service, as he had long planned to do. "As I observed these incidents [Socrates' trial and death] and the men engaged in public affairs," he later said, and

> the more closely I examined them . . . the more difficult it seemed to me to handle public affairs. . . . The result was that, though at first I had been full of a strong impulse towards political life, as I looked at the course of affairs and saw them being swept in all directions by contending currents, my head now began to swim. . . . Finally, it became clear to me with regard to all existing communities, that they were one and all misgoverned. . . . And I was forced to say, when praising true philosophy, that it is by this [i.e., philosophical inquiry] that men are able to see what justice in public and private life really is. Therefore, I said, there will be no cessation of evils . . . till either those who are pursuing . . . philosophy receive sovereign power in the states, or those in power . . . become true philosophers.[35]

Thus, Plato decided that he must devote his life to philosophy, as Socrates had; moreover, he must show his fellow Greeks how to apply philosophy in a practical way, namely, to teach rulers to be just and fair. It seemed to Plato that the first step toward attaining this noble goal was to go out and observe firsthand the way various states were governed. In the years that followed, therefore, he traveled through Greece, visited Egypt, and spent time in the Greek cities of Italy and Sicily.

Eventually, at about the age of forty, Plato returned to Athens. There, he purchased a plot of land and on it founded the world's first university-like school for higher learning—the Academy. He envisioned it primarily as a training ground for a new breed of statesmen—in his view, men of deep personal conviction, commitment to virtue and good works, and a strong sense of justice. He fervently hoped that the school would train the first batch of enlightened rulers whose strong moral compass would help create a better world. Although this dream proved naive, the Academy prospered and survived for some nine hundred years as a world-renowned center of philosophical and other scholarly studies.

Plato's Theory of Forms

During his long tenure as director of the Academy, Plato developed and honed his ideas about the natural world and the human condition. He also turned out many writings on a wide variety of subjects. Central to all of his thinking and writing was his vision of reality, his singular explanation for the underlying principle of nature. It became known as the theory of forms. By "forms," Plato meant ideas or ideal constructions. The physical world perceived by the senses, he said, is in many ways an illusion, as beneath its surface lies an invisible realm of pure ideas. The universe was originally pieced together by a divine craftsman, the Demiurge, who began by constructing all the various objects and elements of Earth and the heavens in perfect forms in his own mind's eye. The visible, touchable versions of these things, said Plato, are only imperfect replicas of the original and ideal forms.

In his famous treatise the *Republic*, the philosopher presented the analogy of a carpenter who visualizes in his mind the bed and table he plans to build. When actually making these items, this craftsman tries as hard as possible to reproduce his mental blueprints of them; however, because of the limitations of his tools, materials, and skills, the finished products do not and can never measure up exactly with his mental pictures. "There are beds and tables in the world—plenty of them," Plato wrote.

> But there are only two ideas or forms of them—one the idea of a bed, the other of a table. . . . And the maker of either of them makes a bed or he makes a table for our use, in accordance with the idea. . . . [The carpenter] cannot make true existence, but only some semblance of existence. . . . God knew this, and he desired to be the real maker of the real bed, not a particular maker of a particular bed, and therefore he created a bed which is essentially and by nature one only.[36]

The major goal of philosophy and science, Plato held, is to seek to understand these perfect, eternal ideas. Only in such understanding will it be possible to comprehend the reality of the natural world.

Eliminating Ignorance Leads to Justice

Although nature's ideal forms are explained in the *Republic*, discussion of them makes up only a small portion of the work. The

44

An engraving shows the gardens adjoining Plato's Academy, located a short distance outside of Athens's urban center.

major theme is justice, which Plato explored by postulating an ideal political state in which the rulers are fair and just. Ordinary men are unfit to rule, he said, because they have not been properly educated, especially in ethics and morality. Only philosophers have been enlightened by the discovery of the true knowledge of moral concepts, especially goodness and justice, and how these should be fairly applied to all members of the community.

To illustrate why philosophers are the best suited of all people to rule, the seventh book of Plato's *Republic* presents a fascinating analogy, usually referred to as the "Myth of the Cave." It is in the form of a dialogue between the characters Socrates and Glaucon. Plato's main thesis is that ordinary people are often politically and intellectually unenlightened. And in the analogy, he likens their state of ignorance to a group of pitiful individuals chained inside of a dark cave. They wrongly assume that the distorted images perceived by their senses in the cave are the real world because they are completely unaware that a wider, well-lit world of "reality" and "truth" exists beyond. Only when a person with a mind trained to see and understand the light (which represents reality and truth) leads them up into the daylight will they, like him, become enlightened. That trained person, of course, is the philosopher. Later in the dialogue, Plato explained that the way to train the mind to see the light is to master subjects that deal with abstract ideas, such as arithmetic,

This well-preserved ancient Roman mosaic depicts Plato and some of his pupils engaged in discussion in the garden of the Academy.

geometry, and astronomy; eventually, the soul will be liberated and capable of comprehending the ideal forms of concepts such as goodness and justice. Thus, Plato concluded, only philosophers, who have achieved true enlightenment, are fit to rule.

The ruling philosopher constitutes only one element of the ideal state Plato described in the *Republic*. Noted classical scholar Michael Grant summarizes the structure of that communistic utopian society:

> Plato's ideal imaginary state is governed by guardians, who are presided over by a "philosophical king" . . . and possess their wives, children, and property in common. There will be three classes of citizens, each performing its proper function, and persuaded to do so, if necessary, by "noble lies." All po-litical change is an illness . . . and educational innovation is wrong, too, since it leads to cultural license—of which po-

etry is an extreme example. . . . Mathematics, on the other hand, provides the ideal subject of instruction.[37]

The Sunken Continent

Plato described a utopian state of a different sort in his treatises titled *Timaeus* and *Critias*. The philosopher claimed that about 590 B.C. his distant ancestor Solon (a noted Athenian lawgiver) had paid a visit to Egypt, where the local priests had told him a fascinating tale. Long ago, they said, Athens had been at war with the people of Atlantis, a huge island or continent lying beyond the Pillars of Heracles (the Greek name for the Strait of Gibraltar, which placed it in the Atlantic Ocean). Then, some nine thousand years before Solon landed in Egypt, an enormous natural disaster had caused the island to sink into the sea and disappear. "Towards the sea, half-way down the length of the whole island," Plato said of Atlantis in *Critias*,

> there was a plain which was said to have been the fairest of all plains and very fertile. Near the plain . . . and also in the center of the island . . . there was a mountain not very high on any side. . . . They had fountains, one of cold and another of hot water, in gracious plenty flowing . . . and there were many temples built and dedicated to many gods. . . . The entire area was densely crowded with habitations; and the canal and the largest of the harbors were

A modern sketch of the metropolis of Atlantis, surrounded by concentric harbors as described in Plato's Critias.

full of vessels and merchants coming from all parts, who, from their numbers, kept up a multitudinous sound of human voices, and a din and clatter of all sorts night and day.[38]

Plato's purpose in telling this tale of a mighty island empire that Athens had defeated in a war and that had then collapsed into the sea was, as in the case of the *Republic*, to provide moral instruction. As scholar J.V. Luce puts it,

> It enabled him to [expound] on the moral corruption introduced by wealth and impiety into the highly civilized commonwealth of Atlantis. He could also praise his own ancestors for their outstanding courage and leadership in his fictitious crisis. In their organization, these proto-Athenians mirror the three classes of the ideal state. There are only 20,000 of them, but they repel the vast hordes of Atlantis.[39]

This moral tale of Plato's was a fiction and no such place as Atlantis ever existed (at least not in 11,000 B.C.!). Yet it appears that he did base some of its events and details on a story (perhaps one indeed collected by his ancestor in Egypt) that told about a real empire and a real natural disaster. A culturally advanced people, the Minoans, had a maritime empire centered in Crete, Greece's largest island, a thousand years before Athens's golden age. Moreover, the central portion of another Minoan island, Thera (lying just north of Crete), collapsed into the sea during a massive volcanic eruption in that same era. Most classical scholars now accept that the story Plato utilized and expanded on in constructing Atlantis was a distorted memory of the Minoans and Thera catastrophe.

Plato's Last Years

Modern experts believe that *Critias* and *Timaeus*, which deal with Atlantis, were written in Plato's later years at the Academy, perhaps when he was in his seventies. It seems that he intended for *Timaeus* to be the first third of a trilogy telling the whole history of the universe and human race up to his time. He failed to finish the second and third installments of the trilogy, however. Instead, he suddenly devoted his full attention to the *Laws*, a large compilation of those statutes he felt would work best in the just and moral state he hoped would emerge in the near future.

A nineteenth-century engraving of the Greek island of Thera. Modern scholars believe that a volcanic catastrophe there inspired the tale of Atlantis's destruction.

No such model state appeared in the few years of life that Plato had left (nor in the long years since his time). Shortly after finishing the work, in about 347 B.C., he passed away at the age of eighty. The exact circumstances of his death are unknown. Popular tradition claims that he attended a wedding feast and fell asleep in his chair, and when his hosts tried to wake him the next morning, they found that he had died peacefully during the night. Plato's ideas did not die, however. The same philosophical questions he asked—including "What is justice?"—continue to be asked today. And his answers still inspire fascination and debate.

CHAPTER 4

Aristotle: How Can Knowledge Be Categorized?

Aristotle was one of the most versatile thinkers who ever lived. Every area of knowledge fascinated him, and he made detailed, logical, and sometimes profound observations in nearly all of these areas. Moreover, he went beyond merely collecting and studying data on various subjects. When he was young, these subjects, including mathematics, physics, ethics, and so forth, were not separate subjects or branches of learning. Rather, all fell under the general heading of philosophy (which still included what today is called science). Aristotle systematized, or categorized, these subjects, becoming the first known scholar to recognize separate branches of learning. He was "the man who established the major and still accepted divisions of philosophy," writes Michael Grant.

> It is from him that philosophers and scientists, of one generation after another, have derived their philosophical terminology which has entered into the inherited vocabulary of educated men and women, so that we employ these terms continually without any longer recalling their source.[40]

Aristotle also provided those seeking knowledge-specific tools to make their job easier. First, he offered what might be called a general theory of knowledge, based on a process of investigation and acquisition of proof. His teacher, Plato, had proposed that the perceived physical world is largely an illusion. Its component objects are imperfect copies of ideal forms existing in an unseen parallel world. Aristotle rejected Plato's forms, saying that there was no need to resort to a mystical realm, the existence of which could not be either proved or disproved. It was better, said Aristotle, to stick with the known world and things that can be seen, touched, and understood in a straightforward manner. (If the forms exist, he said, they lie within the visible objects themselves.) Further, new knowledge and ideas can and should be capable of demonstration. "A truth that is scientifically known does not stand alone," Aristotle's noted modern biographer A.E. Taylor explains.

> The "proof" is simply the pointing out of the connection between the truth we call the conclusion and other truths which we call the premises of our demonstration. Science points out the *reason why* of things, and this is what is meant by the Aristotelian principle that to have science is to know things through their *causes* or *reasons why*.[41]

In addition, Aristotle provided a logical means for discerning the truth of a supposition. He did not invent the discipline of logic. But he was the first thinker to present a systematic explanation of how logic could be used to differentiate between what is valid and what is invalid. He introduced the concept of the syllogism, for example. A syllogism is a kind of argument that tries to prove something through simple deductive reasoning. It consists of three parts: a major premise, a minor premise, and a conclusion that follows logically from the first two parts. Therefore, if premise A and premise B are true, the conclusion, C, which follows from them, must be true, too. For example, if all animals are alive (A), and all dogs are animals (B), then all dogs must be alive (C).

Aristotle, who attempted to categorize knowledge in a systematic way.

Besides systematizing general knowledge and the tools of logic, Aristotle categorized specific branches of learning. In the realm of physics, he listed four "causes," or characteristics, of existence; in his biological writings, he created the world's first classification of the animal kingdom; and in his *Poetics*, he analyzed tragic drama, breaking down a play into its component parts. These and Aristotle's other efforts to systematize knowledge were subjective, based largely on the particular way he saw things. And he was often wrong in the conclusions he drew about people and the natural world. But the mark he left on the field of philosophical-scientific endeavor was simply too enormous for later thinkers and scholars to ignore.

Student and Traveler

Just as Aristotle ended up influencing those scholars who came after him, his own ideas were to a large degree shaped by those of his predecessors. He was born in 384 B.C. at Stagira, a town on the Chalcidic peninsula (on the northern rim of the Aegean Sea). And

Aristotle (right) depicted alongside Plato in Renaissance artist Raphael's famous painting, The School of Athens.

during his boyhood he was most influenced by his father, Nicomachus, a physician to King Amyntas II of Macedonia (in northwestern Greece). At the time, Macedonia was a culturally backward kingdom lying outside the mainstream of Greek affairs, which was centered in Athens, Corinth, Sparta, and the other major city-states of southern Greece. Still, Nicomachus was highly educated and tutored his son in various aspects of philosophy, including the natural sciences, and perhaps also his own vocation, medicine.

In 367 B.C., when Aristotle was seventeen, his father died. His mother had also recently passed away, and the relatives who now had charge of the young man probably recog-

Theophrastus, a close colleague of Aristotle's, was fascinated by plants.

nized that he could not get a decent education in Macedonia. They sent him to Athens, therefore, where he became a student at Plato's Academy. During the twenty years that Aristotle lived at this widely renowned and respected facility, he got to know Plato extremely well. As he matured, the younger man came to disagree with the other on a number of topics (for example, the reality and nature of the forms). Yet the two appear to have shared both friendship and respect. Plato affectionately called Aristotle "the mind" and "the reader," probably references to the younger man's unusual desire and ability to absorb huge amounts of knowledge. That Aristotle looked up to his teacher is revealed by the fact that the young man's earliest written works were dialogues imitating the structure of Plato's famous dialogues.

Whatever the relationship between the two thinkers, it ended abruptly in 347 B.C. with Plato's death. This proved to be a turning point in Aristotle's life. Now in his mid-thirties, he had a respectable position as a researcher and teacher at the Academy. But Plato's nephew, Speusippus, had become director of the facility, and it may well be that Aristotle did not like the way Speusippus ran things. In any case, Aristotle no longer felt comfortable in the place where he had been so happy and productive for more than half of his life, and he decided to leave Athens. (The notion advanced by some scholars, that Aristotle left because he had been passed over for the position of director, is almost certainly wrong. The school and the property on which it sat had belonged to Plato. As a resident alien in Athens, Aristotle was by law barred from owning such property, which naturally passed on to a member of Plato's family.)

Aristotle headed westward across the blue-green waters of the Aegean and for a while settled down in the small Greek town of Assos, on Asia Minor's northwestern coast. There he joined forces with his favorite student from the Academy—Theophrastus (who would later become known as the father of botany). The two men opened a small Academy-like school. But when local politics soon fell under the control of a pro-Persian, anti-Greek faction, Aristotle felt compelled to move again. This time, he and Theophrastus settled on the large Greek island of Lesbos.

It was during this unsettled period in his life that Aristotle married a woman named Pythias. Evidently, he deeply loved and respected her, which says much about his character and ability to express emotion. At the time, most marriages were arranged and romantic love between husband and wife was not the norm. Yet she remained his soul mate, so to speak, even after she died young. Though he went on to marry another woman, Herpyllis, who bore him a son and daughter, he later directed in his will that Pythias's remains be placed beside him in his tomb.

Humans Are Political Animals

During these same years of frequent moving, Aristotle penned some of his more crucial political tracts. Like Plato's *Republic*, Aristotle's *Politics* discusses the characteristics of the ideal political state and community. Aristotle's views on this subject were extremely biased in favor of the Greek states and community life that had nurtured him. For example, he declared that the ideal state for all human beings was the polis, the name the Greeks gave to the city-state, a small nation built around a central city. The main goal of the polis is self-sufficiency (or independence), he wrote. A self-sufficient, self-governing state is natural and affords humans the best chance for leading a good, productive life. Moreover, Aristotle said, "man is by nature an animal designed for living in states." This is sometimes translated as the more familiar "man is by nature a political animal." Humans are unique in this respect, he wrote.

Man is the only animal with the power of speech. . . . Speech is for pointing out what is useful and hurtful; it points out also what is just or unjust. This is peculiar to man. . . . He is the only animal to have a sense of good and evil, just and unjust, and so on.[42]

It is also natural, said Aristotle in the *Politics*, that Greeks should rule over non-Greeks, or "barbarians" (which originally meant

Persian guards carry spears and shields in this bas-relief. Aristotle preached that Persians and other non-Greeks were barbarians.

people who did not speak Greek). This is the result of the Greeks' special combination of intelligence, courage, and spirit. "A natural ruler is not to be found among the barbarians," he claimed.

> Association there is a partnership between slaves, female and male [the first two being plainly inferior to the third]. All the more reason, then, for the poet to say: "It is right for Greeks to rule over barbarians," since barbarian and slave are by nature identical.[43]

From this reasoning, it also followed that slavery is a natural state. "Nature tries to make a difference between slave and free," he declared. "It is clear, then, that people are by nature freemen or slaves, and that it is expedient and just for those who are slaves to be ruled."[44]

Aristotle soon found a young student who avidly believed in these ideas, especially their self-righteous, Greek-centered aspects, and who was eager to apply them in the real political world. During the years when the philosopher was studying and teaching at the Academy, Macedonia had undergone a remarkable transformation. Under a dynamic and ambitious young king, Philip II, the kingdom had become a major political and military power, and it had begun to challenge Athens and the other leading city-states for dominance in the Greek sphere. In 343 B.C. Philip asked Aristotle to come to the Macedonian capital, Pella, and tutor the crown prince. The boy, Alexander III, who would later come to be called "the Great," was then thirteen. Both Philip and Alexander were eager to have the city-states think of them as Greeks. (The propaganda issued by the city-states made the erroneous claim that the Macedonians were uncouth semi-barbarians rather than true Greeks.) They especially wanted to appear as cultured as other Greeks, and the presence at the Macedonian court of Aristotle, a recognized student of the great Plato, elevated their prestige.

Aristotle remained in Macedonia for nearly seven years. He not only reinforced young Alexander's self-identity as a Greek but also instilled in him the notion of natural Greek superiority. The young man soon put his teacher's political ideas into practice. In 336 B.C. an assassin suddenly slew Philip, and Alexander became king of Macedonia. By this time, the kingdom controlled most of Greece (having defeated a coalition of major city-states two years before). Alexander would soon lead the Greeks in a campaign of conquest against the "naturally inferior" Persians.

Aristotle (left) tutors the young Macedonian prince Alexander III in Pella. Alexander later became king and conquered the Persian Empire.

The Structure of the Heavens

In the meantime, with Alexander grown and on the throne, Aristotle was no longer needed in Pella. So the philosopher, now forty-eight, returned to Athens. The following year (335 B.C.), he founded the Lyceum, an institution of higher learning similar to the Academy. (The Lyceum became known as the "peripatetic" school, after the *peripatos*, a pleasant covered walkway used frequently by Aristotle and his students.)

During the next twelve years he spent at the Lyceum, Aristotle turned out most of his important writings. Almost all of these were published. And later ancient scholars, including the noted Roman orator Cicero, praised them as stylish, witty, and thoroughly readable. Unfortunately, the bulk of these published writings are lost. And the massive collection of Aristotle's surviving

In this fanciful drawing, an aged Aristotle walks among animals not native to Greece. One of his major accomplishments was the creation of a zoological classification system.

works is made up primarily of his notes, rough drafts of his lectures, and notes made at his lectures by his students. "Their language," Grant points out, is "dry and formal, and indeed at times pedantic [academic and obscure], so that to read Aristotle is arduous."[45]

However difficult Aristotle's surviving works are to read, they did serve the crucial function of conveying his main ideas to later ages. Of his principal ideas, those dealing with the structure of the cosmos had an especially strong influence on later generations of thinkers, including many scientists. He agreed with Plato and other earlier Greeks that all matter comprises four basic elements—earth, water, air, and fire. In his view, however, these were imperfect and changeable. So they must exist only on Earth. The heavens, in contrast, were permanent and eternal, so they must be made of a special fifth element, which he called the "quintessence" or "ether."

Aristotle also maintained that Earth is a sphere that rests at the center of the universe. He offered two pieces of proof to support these notions. First, falling objects always move toward the center of the planet. Therefore, "its shape must necessarily be spherical," since

> every portion of Earth has weight until it reaches the center. . . . A thing which possesses weight is naturally endowed with a centripetal movement [motion toward a center]. . . . The motions of heavy bodies always make equal angles and are not parallel. This would be the natural form of movement towards what is naturally spherical.[46]

Aristotle's second piece of proof that Earth is round was the fact that the planet casts a curved shadow onto the moon during lunar eclipses. "As it is," he wrote in his treatise *On the Heavens*,

> the shapes which the moon itself each month shows are of every kind—straight, gibbous, and concave—but in eclipses the outline is always curved: and, since it is the interposition of the earth [between sun and moon] that makes the eclipse, the form of this line will be caused by the form of the earth's surface, which is therefore spherical.[47]

Aristotle also wrote extensively about the overall structure of the cosmos. Some earlier Greeks had suggested that the heavens consisted of three large, concentric, and invisible spheres. By the time Aristotle was a young man, the common wisdom was that this basic idea was sound but that there were many more than three cosmic spheres. Eudoxus, a colleague of Plato and Aristotle at the Academy, upped the number to twenty-seven. Each sphere, Eudoxus said, held a planet or other celestial body and accounted for a specific visible motion in the sky. A few years later, Eudoxus's pupil, Callippus, produced a still more complex model having thirty-four heavenly spheres. Aristotle thought that even thirty-four spheres was not enough to explain the complex motions of the heavenly bodies, so he postulated at least fifty-five of these invisible constructions. Although it was eventually proven wrong, Aristotle's version of the spheres and other aspects of his cosmology seemed so logical to so many people that it dominated the field of astronomy for nearly two thousand years.

Exploring the Animal Kingdom

Aristotle's work in biology was ultimately more important than his work in cosmology. This was partly because his ideas about the heavens turned out to be mostly wrong, whereas many of his conclusions about animals and other living things turned out to be right. He collected literally thousands of observations and specimens, which allowed him to launch studies in many areas of biology, including comparative anatomy, ethology (animal habits), embryology (prebirth development), and ecology (relation of animals to their environment). His work in these areas was so fundamental that modern scientists recognize him as the father of biology.

Aristotle studied more than 540 distinct animal species and dissected specimens of at least 50 species. He discovered, among other things, that whales and dolphins are mammals, like people; that some fish have bones and others cartilage; that cows have four-chambered stomachs; that birds and reptiles are anatomically similar; and that embryonic chicks have beating hearts. One of his most famous observations was that of the gestation of a baby chick in its egg. "With the common hen, after three days and three nights there is the first indication of the embryo," he wrote in his *History of Animals*.

> The yoke comes into being, rising towards the sharp end, where the primal element of the egg is situated, and where the egg gets hatched; and the heart appears, like a speck of blood, in the white of the egg. This point beats and moves as though endowed with life. . . . A little afterwards the

The targets of anti-Macedonian sentiments that erupted after the death of Alexander, Aristotle and his followers leave Athens.

body is differentiated . . . [and] when the egg is . . . ten days old the chick and all its parts are distinctly visible.[48]

The most important contribution Aristotle made to the field of biology was his system of zoological classification, which neatly grouped the known animal species by type. He discarded earlier systems that classified species in categories such as land versus water animals, or winged versus wingless creatures. Although a whale lives in water, he pointed out, it is related to land mammals rather than fishes; furthermore, both winged and wingless ants exist. Instead, he divided the animal kingdom into two parts—creatures with blood and those without blood. These two groups further broke down into smaller groups called genera, each genus containing several related species. His five bloodless genera included (in ascending order): zoophytes (corals, sponges), insects, mollusks, crustacea (lobsters, shrimps), and cephalopods (octopi, squids). His six genera having blood were fishes, reptiles and amphibians, birds, sea mammals, land animals, and humans. (Modern biologists also divide the animal kingdom into two main groups—those with and those without backbones. The group with backbones breaks down into several subgroups, including fish, amphibians, reptiles, birds, and mammals; humans, of course, are mammals.)

The Supreme Scholar

As Aristotle studied and wrote about animals, the heavens, and other phenomena at the Lyceum, he could not foresee that events then transpiring in faraway Asia would soon bring his work to an abrupt end. His old pupil Alexander had been busy in recent years. He had defeated and seized the Persian Empire, consisting of all the lands stretching from the Mediterranean coast to distant India. During these same years, Macedonian leaders and supporters had maintained tight control over Greece, causing bitterness and animosity among the city-states. There were rejoicing and rebellion in the Greek city-states, therefore, when the news arrived in 323 B.C. that Alexander had died suddenly (probably of malaria).

Aristotle soon felt himself a target of the anti-Macedonian sentiments raging through southern Greece. Because he had been Alexander's friend and tutor, many Athenians now saw the aging scholar as their enemy. The state put him on trial and, to escape the fate of Socrates, he fled northward to the island of Euboea, where he owned an estate. A few months later (November 322) he passed away there at the age of sixty-two. The Lyceum was clearly in sore need of a new director. Luckily, Aristotle had already expressed his desire that his longtime colleague, Theophrastus, should assume the post; Theophrastus accepted and honored his friend's memory by running the university the same way Aristotle had.

Aristotle's effect on later philosophical and scientific endeavor was both negative and positive. On the negative side, a number of his ideas, including the Earth-centered universe, were incorrect and their almost blind acceptance by later European scholars long impeded progress in astronomy and other disciplines. Indeed, most medieval and early modern scholars saw him as a nearly infallible sage. So they did not attempt to question or further develop his work in logic and the natural sciences.

On the positive side, some of Aristotle's ideas and works, particularly in the field of biology, foreshadowed modern discoveries. He also left behind a means of categorizing knowledge, as his huge intellect sorted through the complexities of nature in search of order and system. For this reason alone, he was the researcher par excellence of premodern times. In Grant's words: "He has been seen throughout the ages as the supreme scholar pursuing the life of the intellect for its own sake; and his posthumous prestige has been more enduring than any other thinker's."[49]

CHAPTER 5

Buddha: Can Suffering Be Overcome?

Today Buddhism, which originated in India and later spread to other lands, is one of the world's great religions. And ample reasons exist to view it as a religion. There are Buddhist priests, temples, and scriptures, for example, and many Buddhists believe in the existence of celestial beings who were once human but managed to attain a higher level of awareness. In these respects, indeed, Buddhism is religious in nature.

However, in its purest form and most basic tenets, Buddhism was and remains a philosophy as well as a religion. In the West, where the vast majority of people know very little about Eastern faiths, many people rather simplistically assume that Buddha must be the god worshiped by Buddhists. In reality, though, Buddhism has no central, all-powerful god. And Siddhārtha Gautama (or Gotama), the man who became known as the Buddha, or "Enlightened One," was just that—a man. (Although this was originally a title, over time people came to see it as his name as well; so the terms "Buddha" and "the Buddha" became interchangeable.) In fact, he made a special point of telling his followers that he was not a divine savior or god. He was merely a thinker and a teacher who had discovered a way to attain true knowledge and peace and who wanted to help others find these things. Even more important, he said, one should not accept things simply as a matter of faith, a practice fundamental to most religions. "Believe nothing just because you have been told it," he said,

> or [because] it is commonly believed, or because it is traditional, or because you yourselves have imagined it. Do not believe what your teacher tells you merely out of respect for the teacher. But whatsoever, after due examination and analysis, you find to be conducive to the good,

the benefit, the welfare of all beings—that doctrine believe and cling to, and take as your guide.[50]

By "that doctrine," Buddha meant the path to knowledge and truth. In most traditional religions, such a path is laid out by a god (or gods), who controls human fate, whereas in Buddhism, the path is discovered by the individual. In Buddha's view, a human being seeks salvation by searching for wisdom. The person hopefully attains that

The renowned statue of Buddha at Kamakura, Japan, was created in 1252, towers 41 feet in height, and weighs 850 tons.

wisdom and thereby becomes the instrument of his or her own fate. Buddha established these and some other simple philosophical beliefs before his later followers added scriptures and various other religious aspects. These basic philosophical tenets were both the driving forces and most bountiful fruits of his life.

The Young and Carefree Prince

As was the case with other ancient religious founders, after Buddha died, a number of the events of his life became exaggerated

An artist's rendition of the miraculous birth of Siddhārtha Gautama, who eventually became known as the Buddha.

and, as time went on, even fabricated and legendary. And it is now impossible to separate reality from legend with any confidence. Still, there seems little doubt that he did exist and that he did, by whatever means, set forth the basic philosophy that ended up inspiring billions of people.

According to Indian tradition, Siddhārtha Gautama was born in northern India in about 563 B.C. His father, Suddhodana, was a local king, as well as a respected leader of the influential Sakya tribe. Later stories claimed that Siddhārtha was conceived miraculously after his mother, Lady Maya, fell asleep and dreamed that she was visited by a sacred white elephant. As written in one of the *Jataka*, a series of birth stories about Buddha compiled in the fifth century A.D.,

> In his [the elephant's] trunk, which was like a silver rope, he held a white lotus. Then, trumpeting, he entered the golden mansion, made a right-wise circle three times around [Maya's] bed, smote [struck] her right side, and appeared to enter her womb.[51]

The next morning the queen awoke and informed the king of her strange dream. He immediately gathered together sixty-four respected holy men and asked them to interpret the dream. The queen had been impregnated, they told the king, with a male child who had two possible futures. If he stayed always in the palace, he would become a great monarch; in contrast, if he went out into the world, he would become a poor monk and hermit.

Suddhodana pondered the situation. That a special child was about to be born seemed certain, for in addition to the queen's dream, a bright light had appeared in the heavens while she was sleeping; moreover, there were reports of deaf people regaining their hearing and physically disabled people who were suddenly able to walk. The problem for the king was the dual prophecy of the holy men. Suddhodana was a rich, worldly man who wanted his son to be an untroubled, happy prince, not a poor, lonely monk. So after Siddhārtha was born, the king made sure that the boy never left the palace grounds. Suddhodana was determined, as Nancy Ross puts it,

> to prevent Siddhartha at all costs from coming in contact with misery or unhappiness in any form. No shadows were to fall on his carefree and gracious existence—shadows that might lead to awkward questions or to painful speculation on life's inequities.[52]

Throughout his youth and young manhood, therefore, Siddhārtha experienced only laughter and good times and knew nothing of the existence of disease, suffering, and death. He married, had a son, and was extremely happy.

Siddhārtha's Disturbing Discovery

When he reached the age of twenty-nine, however, the young prince's happy life changed abruptly. He had always had an inquiring mind and often longed to know about the wider world that lay beyond the palace walls. So one day he and a faithful servant, Channa, secretly escaped into the countryside. It was not long before the two came upon something that Siddhārtha had never seen before—an old man. The dumbfounded prince later recalled thinking,

> I, too, am subject to old age, [and am] not beyond the sphere of old age; and should I, who am subject to old age . . . on seeing an old man, be troubled, ashamed, and disgusted? This seemed to me not fitting. As I thus reflected, all the elation [joy] in [my] youth suddenly disappeared.[53]

Soon, Siddhārtha encountered two other things he viewed as extraordinary and disturbing—a sick person and a dead man being mourned by relatives and friends. The prince asked Channa if such things were common in everyday society, and the servant admitted that illness was very common, while death was inevitable for all people.

Having witnessed the sadder aspects of life, Siddhārtha spent many hours quietly pondering why suffering exists. And because it exists, he wondered, is life even worth living? Then a poor, homeless holy man walked by. Seeing the look of calm on the man's face, the prince suddenly realized that devoting himself to solitude and meditation, as this monk did, might alleviate his growing bewilderment about the world. Siddhārtha also realized that to adopt such a lifestyle would require leaving his family, including his wife and son, whom he dearly loved. So that night he slipped back into the palace. Sadly he gazed down at his wife and son, who were sound asleep, and said his good-byes in silence. He did not wake them, fearing that hearing their voices would cause him to change his mind and stay with them.

After leaving behind his old life, Siddhārtha spent several years attempting to transform himself into an ascetic, a person devoted to a life of extreme self-discipline and self-denial. Month after grueling month, he neglected and punished his body in hopes of

better focusing his mind on finding life's truths. He stopped bathing, pulled the hairs from his head and face one by one, and sometimes lay for hours on beds of thorns. He also sometimes slept among rotting human corpses that had been thrown into a mass grave. Most of all, he practically starved himself, eventually coming to subsist on a single grain of rice per day. He later remembered:

> I thought, what if I were to take food only in small amounts? . . . My body became extremely lean. . . . The bones of my spine, when bent and straightened, were like a row of spindles. . . . As a bitter gourd, cut off raw, is cracked and withered through rain and sun, so was the skin of my head withered through the little [amount of] food [I took in]. When I thought I would touch the skin of my stomach, I actually took hold of my spine.[54]

This starvation approach proved fruitless, however. Despite all his dedication and self-punishment, Siddhārtha found himself unable to discover any great truths or to reach a state of enlightenment. Then it suddenly struck him that abusing his body was pointless and unproductive. Starvation and pain

Siddhārtha (on horse) observes (top to bottom) disability, sickness, death, and a selfless monk.

69

This painting from Tibet shows the angry Mara, goddess of death and desire, trying to stop Buddha from attaining enlightenment.

only succeeded in muddling, rather than sharpening, his thinking. He later told his followers:

> By suffering, the emaciated [extremely thin] devotee produces confusion and sickly thoughts in his mind. Mortification [abuse] is not conducive even to worldly knowledge; how much less to a triumph over the senses! . . . Let [the seeker of wisdom] be moderate, let him eat and drink according to the needs of the body. . . . To keep the body in good health is a duty, for otherwise we shall not be able to trim the lamp of wisdom, and keep our mind strong and clear.[55]

Enlightenment

Now thirty-five, Siddhārtha began eating again. He bathed and donned fresh, clean clothes, too. When he had regained his health, he set out with a clear mind and renewed determination to find the source of human suffering. Sometime in May 528 B.C., he came upon a banyan tree (in some versions a fig tree) and sat down beside it to meditate. (This later became renowned and revered as the Bodhi Tree, or "Tree of Wisdom.")

As the man meditated, he felt he was seeing things more clearly than ever before. The concepts of sorrow, sickness, old age, and death swirled through his mind, which examined each, along with its consequences, in a cool, dispassionate manner. "With mind concentrated, purified, cleansed," he later recalled,

Buddha achieves enlightenment and contemplates the four great truths.

I directed my mind to the passing away and rebirth of things. [With] purified vision, I saw beings passing away and being reborn, low and high . . . in happy or miserable existences . . . according to that universal law by which every act of good or evil will be rewarded or punished in this life or in some later incarnation of the soul.[56]

No one knows how long Siddhārtha sat there in his trance; it may have been a few days or many days. Later stories claimed that Mara, an evil being, recognized that the man was on the brink of acquiring wisdom and sought to divert him. In one version, Mara tempted him with earthly pleasures; in another story, the evil one sent storms to disrupt the man's concentration.

But nothing could deflect Siddhārtha from his chosen path. On May 25, 528 B.C., he opened his eyes, having at last reached the end of his fateful intellectual journey. He had learned the cause of human suffering, and thereby he had attained enlightenment and become the Buddha.

The Eightfold Path

Buddha now knew what he must do. Once more, he put a major part of his life behind him; from that day forward, he made it his mission to help others understand the truths he had come to recognize. As his first converts soon discovered, these truths are four in number. The first is self-evident, namely, that life is filled with suffering. The second truth is that human suffering is the result of conceit, self-indulgence, greed, and possessiveness; as people tend to think mainly of their own comforts and become preoccupied with material possessions, they give too little thought to alleviating poverty and treating everyone justly. Buddha's third truth is that these ills are not inevitable, as people so often assume; they *can* be overcome.

Finally, Buddha revealed a fourth truth, perhaps the most important of all. It consists of the means of overcoming the causes of suffering, a code of conduct he called the Eightfold Path. Briefly summarized, the eight steps are right views (or understanding), right aspiration (or purpose), right speech, right behavior, right vocation (or livelihood), right effort, right thoughts (or awareness), and right contemplation (or concentration, or meditation). In Buddha's own words, the enlightened person "will walk in the right path" in which

right views will be the torch to light his way. Right aspirations will be his guide. Right speech will be his dwelling-place on the road. His gait will be straight because it is

72

Siddhārtha (riding in carriage) sees a dead person (lying among mourners at right). Before witnessing this scene of mourning, the prince had led a sheltered life.

right behavior. His refreshments will be the right way of earning his livelihood. Right efforts will be his steps. Right thoughts his breath. And right contemplation will give him the peace that follows in his footprints.[57]

Thus, a person should think and speak truthfully; set moral, constructive goals; behave in an honest, just manner; earn a living in a way that does not hurt others; and periodically reevaluate his or her life through meditation. According to Buddha, he or she can then attain Nirvana, a state of selflessness, peace, and bliss.

Although Buddha's disciples saw the inherent wisdom of the Eightfold Path, some pointed out that its steps all emphasize what one should *do*. And they asked him to give some specific examples of what one should *not do*. Buddha responded by listing what became known as the Five Moral Rules. These are

1. Let not one kill any living thing.

2. Let not one take what is not given him.

3. Let not one speak falsely.

4. Let not one drink intoxicating drinks.

5. Let not one be unchaste [sexually impure].[58]

An Emphasis on Conduct

With his unique philosophy in place, Buddha began preaching. And his reputation quickly grew. As he traveled through the Indian countryside, he gained new converts wherever he went and sometimes hundreds of people followed him from place to place. There are stories about his performing supernatural feats during his ministry. In one, Buddha transported himself though the air across the Ganges River; in another, he dropped a toothpick, which imbedded itself in the ground and rapidly grew into a tree. It was also said that Earth and the heavens trembled following one of his sermons.

These stories were surely created after Buddha's death. He himself scorned the idea of humans performing miracles. In fact, he would not have approved of his later disciples' elevation of both him and his teachings onto a mystical, religious level. "His conception of religion was purely ethical," noted historian Will Durant points out in this informative passage:

> He cared everything about conduct, nothing about ritual or worship . . . or theology. . . . There is nothing stranger in the history of religion than the sight of Buddha founding a worldwide religion, and yet refusing to be drawn into any discussion about eternity, immortality, or God. The infinite is a myth, he says, a fiction of philosophers who have not the modesty to confess that an atom can never understand the cosmos. . . . He denounces the notion of sacrificing to the gods, and looks with horror upon the slaughter of animals for these rites; he rejects all cult and worship of supernatural beings . . . all asceticism and all prayer.[59]

For someone to profess such beliefs in those days was highly unusual. After all, almost all Indians followed Hinduism, a religion that accepted the idea of multiple gods who could and did come to Earth and perform miracles. (Hinduism eventually recognized Buddha as a great teacher.) Yet many of Buddha's followers had no problem reconciling his philosophical ideas about right living and meditation with existing Hindu doctrines. Contributing to this commingling of the two doctrines was the fact that Buddha had borrowed a number of Hindu terms and concepts, including Nirvana, in constructing his philosophical worldview.

Decay Is a Part of Life

As Buddha and his initial disciples spread this new philosophy far and wide, they eventually arrived in the kingdom in which long ago he had been born a prince named Siddhārtha. Hearing that he was in the area, his father, the king, sent an invitation for the great thinker to visit his old home. Buddha happily accepted and greeted his family warmly. King Suddhodana admitted that once he had been reluctant to see his son become a holy man, but now he was proud to be the father of one of India's greatest sages.

Then Buddha's former wife threw herself at his feet as if he were a god. He bade her stand, for he was no god, he said, only a man. The king then told his son how this woman, out of her deep love for the former Siddhārtha, had tried to imitate his modest lifestyle. "Lord," said Suddhodana,

> my daughter-in-law, when she heard that you were wearing yellow robes [traditional monkish attire], put on yellow robes; when she heard of your having one meal a day, she too took one meal; when she knew that you had given up a large bed, she lay on a narrow couch.[60]

As for Buddha's son, now a young man, he willingly gave up his chance to become king someday and eagerly joined his father's new order.

Buddha continued teaching for many years to come. Eventually, in 483 B.C., when he was eighty, he sensed that he was dying. He urged those followers who had gathered around his bedside not to waste a lot of time mourning his passing; rather, they should accept his death, like the deaths of all people, as part of the great wheel of life. Further, they should concentrate their time and energy on spreading knowledge about suffering and how to overcome it. His last words were reportedly: "Decay is inherent in all things. Work out your own salvation with diligence."[61] This reinforced his doctrine that each individual's fate lies ultimately in his or her own thoughts and actions. Since the day of Buddha's death, countless people in many parts of the globe have taken these and his other words to heart.

CHAPTER 6

Confucius: How Should People Treat One Another?

Confucius said: "He who learns but does not think is lost. He who thinks but does not learn is in great danger."[62] This is how most Westerners know the Chinese thinker Confucius—as the source of a series of short pithy sayings about life. These sayings, the *Analects* (meaning "fragments"), were collected from memory by some of his immediate followers following his death, and they constitute the most reliable surviving guide to his philosophy.

That philosophy, which contains much more than mere witty sayings, was unusual in the East for its worldliness and secularism (nonspirituality). Most of the respected Eastern thinkers tended to reject worldly lives in favor of monklike solitude, poverty, meditation, and spirituality. In contrast, Confucius was a social and political figure, a civil servant who sought to reform the ills of society and government by encouraging people, especially leaders, to be honest and ethical. As noted scholar Lin Yutang explains,

> Confucianism stood for a rationalized social order through the ethical approach, based on personal cultivation. It aimed at political order by laying the basis for it in a moral order. . . . Thus, its most curious characteristic was the abolition of the distinction between politics and ethics. . . . Fundamentally, it was a humanist attitude, brushing aside all futile metaphysics [supernaturalism] and mysticism, interested chiefly in the essential human relationships, and not in the world of spirits or in immortality.[63]

Thus, Confucius laid the responsibility for maintaining good government and a humane society on the individual. The key was good morals and good behavior, which he held sprang from simple learning and respect for tradition, rather than from divinely inspired ideals. At the very core of Confucius's thinking was the golden rule. "Do not do to others what you would not like [done to] yourself," he said. "Then there will be no feelings of opposition to you, whether it is in the affairs of a state . . . or the affairs of a family."[64]

Perhaps no other single ancient philosophy has so directly affected the daily lives of so many people as that advocated by Confucius. In the centuries following his death, increasing numbers of people, including political leaders, adopted his ideas. His secular code of ethics came to coexist alongside the spiritual tenets of religions like Buddhism and Taoism and over time helped to mold the character of the Chinese people. Confucius's ideas, writes scholar Liu Wu-Chi,

The Chinese thinker Confucius, who advocated that politicians act ethically.

> have been formulated since his day into a governing code of etiquette and morality for all the Chinese. . . . In almost everything from their national to private life, in their culture, in their manners and behavior, in their customs and traditions . . . the Chinese have been greatly indebted to Confucius. It is no

exaggeration, then, to say that it is his teachings that have welded together the Chinese nation.[65]

Birth and Childhood

Perhaps partly because Confucius dealt directly with political problems and interacted with famous rulers, more is known about his life than about the lives of other ancient Eastern thinkers. Later generations desiring to know about his life certainly owe a debt to Szema Ch'ien. The greatest of ancient Chinese historians, he was born around 145 B.C., less than four centuries after Confucius died, and wrote a biography of him that has survived. The authority of this work "is unquestioned," Lin Yutang points out.

Ch'ien himself traveled extensively and visited the birthplace of Confucius and talked with old people who kept

Young Chinese students learn about Confucius's ideas, which have become integrated into nearly every aspect of Chinese life.

Confucius establishes his school, where students studied history, poetry, and ethics. Many of his pupils became dedicated followers.

alive the ancient tradition about Confucius. It is therefore as accurate a picture of Confucius's life as we can get.[66]

According to Szema Ch'ien, Confucius was born in 551 B.C. in Tsou, a town in the kingdom of Lu, now part of China's Shantung province. His birth name was K'ung Ch'iu. The name Confucius is a slurred Western pronunciation of K'ung Fu-tzu, meaning

This work by an unknown Chinese artist shows scholars finding manuscripts of Confucius's teachings that had been concealed in a wall.

"K'ung the Master," the appellation of respect given to the philosopher by his first disciples.

Confucius's father was Shuliang Ho, a farmer of modest means. When he was a young man, Shuliang Ho had an affair with a young woman named Yen Chentsai, who became pregnant; because they were not married, the baby—Confucius —was illegitimate. Not long after the boy's birth, his father died. And because the parents were not living together, Shuliang Ho was buried in another town (Fangshu). "Therefore," as Szema Ch'ien told it, when Confucius became a young man, he

> was in doubt as to the place of his father's tomb, because his mother had concealed the truth from him. When he was a child, he used to play at making sacrificial offerings and performing the [funeral] ceremonies. When Confucius's mother died, he buried her temporarily . . . in the street of the Five Fathers, and it was not until an old woman . . . informed him of the whereabouts of his father's grave, that he buried his parents together at Fangshu.[67]

While his mother was still living, young Confucius did odd jobs after school each day to help her pay the bills. A very serious student, he studied hard and read a lot. Still, he enjoyed sports, especially fishing and shooting the bow and arrow, as well as music. At the age of nineteen, the young man married, but for reasons that are now unclear, the union did not last long. It did produce one child—a son named K'ung Li (referred to as Po Yu in the *Analects*).

The Way to Reform Society

Confucius's diligence in his studies as a child and teenager eventually paid off. By the time he was twenty-two, he was already well known throughout the realm of Lu as an unusually wise, honest, and upright person. He decided to establish a school and immediately began to attract students. Like Plato's Academy and Aristotle's Lyceum, which would be founded in Greece more than a century later, it taught traditional subjects such as history, poetry, and ethics in hopes of turning out well-rounded individuals who could go on to affect society in positive ways.

Confucius wanted to emphasize the positive because he was worried that both society and government in China were becoming lax, corrupt, and detrimental to the needs and well-being of the people. The most obvious aspect of this disturbing situation was corrupt or neglectful rulers. But in Confucius's view, this was more a symptom than a cause of the problem. Bad rulers are not good people who suddenly become corrupt when they enter public service, he said, but rather the product of an impaired social system that nurtures them and shapes their morals. Thus, to eliminate corruption and immorality at the top, one must examine and reform the entire system from the bottom up, beginning with the family and its individual members.

This reform involves a search for wisdom, Confucius said. If one accumulates knowledge, especially about time-honored traditions and morality, he reasoned, one will become and remain honest and good. And that goodness will filter up through society to the highest levels. The essence of these ideas was captured in the following crucial statement attributed to Confucius by one of his followers:

> Wishing to be sincere in their thoughts, [our ancient forefathers] first extended to the utmost their knowledge. . . . Their knowledge being complete, their thoughts were sincere . . . [and] their hearts were then rectified . . . their own selves were cultivated . . . their families were regulated . . . [and] their states were rightly governed.[68]

The great modern scholar Will Durant offers this excellent interpretation of the passage and its philosophy:

> [Countries] are improperly governed because no amount of legislation can take the place of the natural social order provided by the family; the family is in disorder, and fails to provide this natural social order, because men forget that they cannot regulate their families if they do not regulate themselves. . . . Their thinking is insincere because they let their wishes discolor the facts and determine their conclusions. . . . Let them seek impartial knowledge, and their thinking will become sincere. . . . Let their own selves be regulated, and their families will automatically be regulated. . . . Let the family be so regulated with knowledge, sincerity, and example, and it will give forth such spontaneous social order that successful government will once more be a feasible thing.[69]

Thus, moral clarity, good government, and a happy society ultimately derive from the search for knowledge, which imparts wisdom.

The Lady and the Tiger

Confucius was glad to see many of his students eagerly embrace this philosophy that morality must be nurtured at all levels of

Confucius (in wagon) was appalled by the violence and disorder in a number of Chinese states. He felt that bad govenment was to blame.

society. Some of these young men graduated from his school and gained responsible government positions. They continued educating themselves and were honest and forthright in their dealings, with the result that the quality of government in Lu began to increase. Confucius became so respected that a powerful duke expressed a deathbed wish that his son go to study with the philosopher. In this way, Confucius gained the prestigious reputation of an instructor of princes.

In 517 B.C., however, the philosopher experienced a sudden change of fortune. Some powerful chieftains of Lu had a falling-out with Duke Chao, the reigning ruler of the kingdom, who was also a friend and patron of Confucius. Violence erupted and the duke soon faced a choice between complete defeat and flight. He chose the latter. Though the philosopher could have remained in the capital and continued teaching there, out of loyalty he chose to go with Duke Chao into exile in the neighboring kingdom of Ch'i.

On the way to Ch'i, the party had an experience, now quite famous in Asia, that demonstrated Confucius's wisdom in two ways. On the one hand, it showed that he was correct in his view that the people needed and longed for fair government. It also showed Confucius's practical and persuasive method of teaching. Along a mountain trail, the travelers suddenly heard a woman crying nearby. They investigated and found a young woman weeping beside a grave. Confucius asked a soldier to question the woman, who explained, "First my father-in-law was killed here by a tiger; then my husband met the same fate; and now death has come [in the same manner] to my son!" When the soldier asked why she and her family had not moved away from this tiger-infested region, she said, "There is no oppressive government here." Hearing this, Confucius told his fellow travelers, "My children, remember this: An oppressive government is fiercer than a tiger."[70]

The Golden Age

Just such a bad government had taken control of Lu after Duke Chao's flight. Fighting among the chieftains continued even after Chao died in exile six years later. Meanwhile, Confucius had decided to return to his homeland. Seeing that the kingdom was wracked by political chaos, for a while he carefully avoided the court and concentrated on his teaching.

Eventually, though, a new duke, named Ting, asked the philosopher to become actively engaged in government service. In 501 B.C., Confucius, now about fifty, took charge of the important town of Chungtu. He did such a good job that Duke

An artist's rendition of Confucius's tomb. Today, the spot is marked by a grassy mound and a tall, rectangular stone slab.

Ting promoted him to the position of minister of public works for all of Lu. In the short span of four years, Confucius rose even higher in the government, becoming the minister of justice and finally the prime minister. In this last office, the philosopher performed so many crucial duties and earned so much respect that he wielded more authority over everyday affairs than the duke himself.

As prime minister, Confucius wasted no time in translating his philosophy of honest government into reality. Whenever possible, he fired corrupt or wasteful officials and replaced them with his own students, who implemented his ideas. The result was a brief moment in Chinese history that later generations would look back on as a sort of golden age. According to Szema Ch'ien,

> Butchers did not adulterate [add scraps to] their meat. . . . Things lost on the streets were not stolen, and foreigners visiting the country did not have to go to the police, but all came to Lu like a country of their own [i.e., felt as safe and comfortable there as they did at home].[71]

This was a welcome turn of events in Lu, but the leaders of neighboring lands became worried. The advisers of the ruler of Ch'i, for example, told him: "If Confucius remains in power in Lu, Lu is certain to dominate the other states."[72] So the ruler of Ch'i devised a plan to cause trouble between Confucius and Duke Ting. One day word arrived in the capital of Lu that a magnificent present was on its way from the court of Ch'i to Ting's own court. Confucius discovered that the gift consisted of eighty beautiful women and 120 horses. He realized that if Ting accepted the gift, the duke would be so distracted from his governmental duties that the kingdom would surely suffer. So the prime minister ordered the men bearing the women and horses to remain outside the capital. Ting could not resist the temptation, however. He sent soldiers to bring the gift to him and soon incorporated the women into his harem. Sure enough, the duke began to shirk his duties and became a very neglectful and un-Confucian ruler. Confucius protested in a way that surprised everyone; he resigned his post as prime minister and went into voluntary exile.

The Final Wanderings

Confucius now wandered through China for no less than thirteen years. Accompanied by a few of his closest disciples, he spent time in the neighboring states of Wei, Ch'en, Sung, and Chin. All of the rulers and officials in these lands knew of the philosopher-politician's reputation, but most of them were reluctant to give him a position of authority. Like the leaders of Ch'i, they worried that he might only end up causing trouble. But Confucius refused to despair. He was supremely confident in his ability to implement his ideas and bring about positive change. "If only someone were to make use of me [as a public official], even for a single year," he declared, "I could do a great deal. And in three years, I could finish off the whole work [and make that government perfect]."[73]

Confucius's long exile ended in 484 B.C., when he was in his late sixties. Duke Ting had died some years before, and the kingdom of Lu was now ruled by Duke Gae. Gae sent the philosopher an invitation to return to his homeland once more. And Confucius thankfully accepted. During the five years that followed, he spent most of his time enjoying a quiet existence in which he did much writing, including a history of his people. From time to time, government ministers paid visits to the aging thinker, and he graciously gave them political advice. Most of all, he continued to stress the golden rule, pointing out that all people should treat others as they themselves would want to be treated.

One day in 479 B.C., when he was seventy-three, Confucius grew very weak and realized that death was near. He put his affairs in order and told his disciples, "No intelligent monarch arises. There is not one in the empire who will make me his master. My time has come to die."[74] Then he lay down on a couch and rested for seven days, after which he died peacefully. His closest followers buried him in a reverent ceremony and erected small huts near the grave. All but one of them dwelled in these humble shelters for three years, mourning their master all day, every day. The one exception was Tsze-kung, who had been the closest of all to Confucius. After the others departed, Tsze-kung stayed and mourned another three years.

It turned out that Confucius's greatest tribute was not how much people missed him after his passing, but how strongly they embraced his ideas in the generations to come. Only three centuries later, Szema Ch'ien wrote:

> There have been many kings, emperors, and great men in history, who enjoyed fame and honor while they lived and came to nothing at their death, while Confucius, who was but a common scholar clad in a cotton gown, became the acknowledged Master of scholars for over ten generations. All people in China . . . from the emperors, kings, and princes down, regard the Master as the final authority.[75]

Democritus on Good Government

This collection of some of the surviving fragments of Democritus's writings conveys his general view that fair, constructive government, preferably democratic in nature, is essential to the well-being of the community.

Quoted in Jonathan Barnes, *Early Greek Philosophy*. New York: Penguin, 1987, p. 277.

Poverty in a democracy is preferable to what is called prosperity among tyrants—by as much as liberty is preferable to slavery.

One should think it of greater moment than anything else that the affairs of the state are conducted well, neither being contentious beyond what is proper nor allotting strength to oneself beyond the common good. For a state which is conducted well is the best means to success: everything depends on this, and if this is preserved everything is preserved and if this is destroyed everything is destroyed.

It is not advantageous for good men to neglect themselves and look to other things; for their own affairs will go badly. But if anyone neglects public affairs he comes to have a bad reputation, even if he steals nothing and commits no injustice. For even if he takes care and does no wrong, there is still a danger that he will get a bad reputation—and indeed fare badly: wrong-doing is inevitable and forgiveness is not easy for men.

When bad men gain office, the more unworthy they are the more heedless they become and the more they are filled with folly and rashness.

When those in power take it upon themselves to lend to the poor and to aid them and to favour them, then is there pity and no isolation but companionship and mutual defence and concord among the citizens and other good things too many to catalogue.

Democritus

Plato Explores the Nature of Justice
In this excerpt from the first book of his *Republic*, Plato tries to establish that a just person will be happier in life than an unjust person.

As in his other dialogues, he uses the Socratic method. The questioner (Socrates, whom Plato often used for this role) asks a friend named Thrasymachos a series of questions designed to lead him to a logical conclusion.

Plato, *Republic*, in *Great Dialogues of Plato*. Trans. W.H.D. Rouse. New York: New American Library, 1956, pp. 152–54.

"We now come to the second question which we proposed. Have the just a better life of it than the unjust? Are they happier? Indeed they appear to be so already, as I think, from what we have said, but let us examine still more carefully. The matter is no chance trifle, but how we ought to live."

"Examine away," said he.

"Here goes then," said I. "Kindly tell me—do you think a horse has his work?"

"I do."

"Then would you put down as the work of a horse, or anything else, that which you could do only with the thing, or best with it?" . . . [After giving it some thought, Thrasymachos agrees.]

"Very good," said I. "Do you think there is a virtue in each thing which has a work appointed for it? Let us run over the same things. Eyes, we say, have a work?"

"They have."

"Then have eyes a virtue too?"

"They have a virtue too."

"Well, the ears had a work?"

"Yes."

"And a virtue too?"

"True."

"But what about all the other things? Does not the same hold good?"

"It does."

"One moment, now. Could the eyes do their work well if they had not their own proper virtue, but instead of the virtue a vice?"

"How could they?" he said—"I suppose you mean blindness instead of sight."

"Which is their virtue," I said, "but I do not ask that yet; I ask if their proper virtue makes them do well the work which they do, and vice makes them do it badly?"

"That is true so far," he said.

"Then ears also, deprived of their own virtue, will do their work badly."

"Certainly."

"Do we say the same of all the other things?"

"I think so."

"Consider the next point, then. Soul has a work, which you could not do with anything else? Something of this sort; to care, to rule, to plan, and all things like that. Is there anything but soul to which we could tightly entrust them and say they are its own?"

"Nothing else."

"What, again, of life? Shall we say it is a work of soul?"

"Most certainly," said he.

"And do we not say that soul has a virtue also?"

"Yes."

"Then will soul ever do its work well, Thrasymachos, deprived of its proper virtue? Is that not impossible?"

"Impossible."

"A bad soul then must needs rule and care badly, but a good soul must needs do all these things well."

"It must needs be so."

"Now did we not agree that soul's virtue was justice, and soul's vice injustice?"

"We did."

"Then the just soul and the just man will live well, and the unjust man badly."

"So it appears by your reasoning."

"But, further, he who lives well is blessed and happy, he that does not is the opposite."

"Of course."

"The just man then is happy, and the unjust miserable."

"Let it be so," he said.

"But to be miserable is not profitable, to be happy, is."

"Of course."

"Then, O Thrasymachos, blessed among men! injustice is never more profitable than justice!"

Plato

Aristotle Concludes That Slavery Is Natural

Like nearly all ancients, Aristotle took the institutions of male dominance and slavery for granted, as revealed in this passage from his *Politics*, in which he explains why he sees them as perfectly natural and acceptable.

Aristotle, *Politics*, excerpted in Renford Bambrough, ed., *The Philosophy of Aristotle*. New York: New American Library, 1963, pp. 388–89.

As regards male and female, the former is superior, the latter inferior; the male is ruler, the female is subject. It must also be that the same is true for the whole of mankind. Where there is a difference between people, like that between soul and body, or between man and mere animal (this being the condition of people whose function is to use their bodies, manual labor being the best service they can give, for such people are by nature slaves), it is better for the lower ones to be ruled, just as it is for the subjects mentioned above. A man is a slave by nature if he *can* belong to someone else (this is why he does in fact belong to someone else) or if he has reason to the extent of understanding it without actually possessing it. Animals other than man do not obey reason, but follow their instincts. There is only a slight difference between the services rendered by slaves and by animals: both give assistance with their bodies for the attainment of the essentials of living.

Nature tries to make a difference between slave and free, even as to their bodies—making the former strong, with a view to their doing the basic jobs, and making the free people upright, useless for servile jobs but suitable for political life, which is divided into the tasks of war and of peace. The opposite, however, often turns out to be the case: it happens that some have the physique of free men, whereas others have the souls. It is quite obvious that if people showed their differences in their mere physique, as the statues of the gods show the difference between gods and men, everyone would say that the inferior ones ought to be slaves of the others.

If this is true of the body, it is even more just for the distinction to apply to the soul. But it is not so easy to see the beauty of the soul as the beauty of the body. It is clear, then, that people are by nature free men or slaves, and that it is expedient and just for those who are slaves to be ruled.

Aristotle

Buddha Condemns Evildoers

This passage is from the *Dhammapada*, or "Words and Doctrine," a volume of verses composed by an unknown later disciple of Buddha, who attributed their basic content to Buddha himself. The message of the passage is plain: evil will destroy the evildoer as well as his or her victims.

Quoted in Lin Yutang, ed., *The Wisdom of China and India*. 1942. Reprint, New York: Random House, 1955, pp. 335–36.

A MAN should hasten towards the good, and should keep his thought away from evil; if a man does what is good slothfully, his mind delights in evil.

If a man commits a sin, let him not do it again; let him not delight in sin: the accumulation of evil is painful.

If a man does what is good, let him do it again; let him delight in it: the accumulation of good is delightful.

Even an evil-doer sees happiness so long as his evil deed does not ripen; but when his evil deed ripens, then does the evil-doer see evil.

Even a good man sees evil days so long as his good deed does not ripen; but when his good deed ripens, then does the good man see good things.

Let no man think lightly of evil, saying in his heart, It will not come nigh unto me. Even by the falling of water-drops a water-pot is filled; the fool becomes full of evil, even if he gather it little by little.

Let no man think lightly of good, saying in his heart, It will not come nigh unto me. Even by the falling of water-drops a water-pot is filled; the wise man becomes full of good, even if he gather it little by little.

Let a man avoid evil deeds, as a merchant, if he has few companions and carries much wealth, avoids a dangerous road; as a man who loves life avoids poison.

He who has no wound on his hand, may touch poison with his hand; poison does not affect one who has no wound; nor is there evil for one who does not commit evil.

If a man offend a harmless, pure, and innocent person, the evil falls back upon that fool, like light dust thrown up against the wind.

Some people are born again; evil-doers go to hell; righteous people go to heaven; those who are free from all worldly desires attain Nirvāna.

Not in the sky, not in the midst of the sea, not if we enter into the clefts of the mountains, is there known a spot in the whole world where a man might be freed from an evil deed.

Not in the sky, not in the midst of the sea, not if we enter into the clefts of the mountains, is there known a spot in the whole world where death could not overcome the mortal.

Attributed to Buddha

Confucius Promotes the Golden Mean

Many of the ideas and sayings recorded by Confucius's early followers were attributed to him, or at least purported to capture the spirit of his thinking. This passage is from the *Central Harmony*, often called "The Golden Mean," thought to have been compiled by Confucius's grandson, Tsesze. The central harmony, or golden mean, is a universal moral order that all people are urged to discover and follow.

Quoted in Lin Yutang, ed., *The Wisdom of Confucius.* 1938. Reprint, New York: Modern Library, 1994, pp. 105–7.

Confucius remarked: "The life of the moral man is an exemplification of the universal moral order. The life of the vulgar person, on the other hand, is a contradiction of the universal moral order.

The moral man's life is an exemplification of the universal order, because he is a moral person who unceasingly cultivates his true self or moral being. The vulgar person's life is a contradiction of the universal order, because he is a vulgar person who in his heart has no regard for, or fear of, the moral law."

Confucius remarked: "To find the central clue to our moral being which unites us to the universal order, that indeed is the highest human attainment. For a long time, people have seldom been capable of it."

Confucius remarked: "I know now why the moral life is not practiced. The wise mistake moral law for something higher than what it really is; and the foolish do not know enough what moral law really is. I know now why the moral law is not understood. The noble natures want to live too high, high above their moral ordinary self; and ignoble natures do not live high enough, i.e., not up to their moral ordinary true self. There is no one who does not eat and drink. But few there are who really know flavor."

Confucius remarked: "There is in the world now really no moral social order at all."

Confucius remarked: "Men all say 'I am wise'; but when driven forward and taken in a net, a trap, or a pitfall, there is not one who knows how to find a way of escape. Men all say, 'I am wise'; but in finding the true central clue and balance in their moral being, they are not able to keep it for a round month." . . .

Confucius remarked: "A man may be able to put a country in order, be able to spurn the honors . . . office, be able to trample upon bare, naked weapons: with all that he is still not able to find the central clue in his moral being."

Tselu asked what constituted strength of character.

Confucius said: "Do you mean strength of character of the people of the southern countries or force of character of the people of the northern countries; or do you mean strength of character of your type? To be patient and gentle, ready to teach, returning not evil for evil: that is the strength of character of the people of the southern countries. It is the ideal place for the moral man. To lie under arms and meet death without regret; that is the strength of character of the people of the northern countries. It is the ideal of brave men of your type. Wherefore the man with the true strength of moral character is one who is gentle, yet firm. How unflinching is his strength! When there is moral social order in the country, if he enters public life he does not change from what he was when in retirement. When there is no moral social order in the country, he is content unto death. How unflinching is his strength!"

Confucius remarked: "There are men who seek for the abstruse and strange and live a singular life in order that they may leave a name to posterity. This is what I never would do. There are again good men who try to live in conformity with the moral law, but who, when they have gone half way, throw it up. I never could give it up. Lastly, there are truly moral men who unconsciously live a life in entire harmony with the universal moral order and who live unknown to the world and unnoticed of men without any concern. It is only men of holy, divine natures who are capable of this."

Attributed to Confucius

NOTES

Introduction: Men Who Asked, "What, Why, and How?"

1. Bertrand Russell, *A History of Western Philosophy.* New York: Simon and Schuster, 1972, pp. xiii–xiv.

2. Quoted in Frank N. Magill, ed., *Masterpieces of World Philosophy.* New York: HarperCollins, 1990, p. viii.

Chapter 1: The Development of Ancient Philosophy

3. E.W.F. Tomlin, *The Oriental Philosophers: An Introduction.* New York: Harper and Row, 1963, p. 21.

4. Tomlin, *Oriental Philosophers,* p. 20.

5. Lucretius, *The Nature of the Universe,* trans. Ronald Latham. Baltimore: Penguin, 1951, p. 29.

6. Jonathan Barnes, *Early Greek Philosophy.* New York: Penguin, 1987, pp. 13–14.

7. Quoted in Philip Wheelwright, ed., *The Presocratics.* New York: Macmillan, 1966, pp. 46–47.

8. Quoted in Wheelwright, *Presocratics,* p. 58.

9. Quoted in Wheelwright, *Presocratics,* pp. 160–61.

10. Quoted in Wheelwright, *Presocratics,* p. 213.

11. John M. Koller, *Asian Philosophies.* Englewood Cliffs, NJ: Prentice-Hall, 2002, pp. 9–10.

12. Quoted in Nancy W. Ross, *Three Ways of Asian Wisdom.* New York: Simon and Schuster, 1978, p. 81.

13. Ross, *Three Ways of Asian Wisdom,* p. 140.

14. Ross, *Three Ways of Asian Wisdom,* p. 148.

Chapter 2: Democritus: What Is Nature's Underlying Structure?

15. Diogenes Laertius, *Lives of Eminent Philosophers.* Trans. R.D. Hicks. 2 vols. Cambridge: Harvard University Press, 1995, vol. 2, p. 447.

16. Diogenes Laertius, *Lives,* vol. 2, p. 451.

17. Diogenes Laertius, *Lives,* vol. 2, p. 455.

18. Quoted in Wheelwright, *Presocratics,* p. 186.

19. Diogenes Laertius, *Lives*, vol. 2, p. 445.

20. Quoted in Barnes, *Early Greek Philosophy*, p. 244.

21. Diogenes Laertius, *Lives*, vol. 2, p. 447.

22. Quoted in Barnes, *Early Greek Philosophy*, p. 248.

23. Quoted in Barnes, *Early Greek Philosophy*, p. 255.

24. Quoted in Wheelwright, *Presocratics*, pp. 189–90.

25. Quoted in Barnes, *Early Greek Philosophy*, p. 244.

26. Quoted in Barnes, *Early Greek Philosophy*, p. 277.

27. Quoted in Barnes, *Early Greek Philosophy*, pp. 260–61.

28. Diogenes Laertius, *Lives*, vol. 2, p. 449.

29. Diogenes Laertius, *Lives*, vol. 2, p. 453.

30. Quoted in Barnes, *Early Greek Philosophy*, pp. 273, 257.

Chapter 3: Plato: What Is the Meaning of Justice?

31. Alfred North Whitehead, *Process and Reality: An Essay in Cosmology.* Ed. D.R. Griffin and D.W. Sherburne. New York: Free Press, 1978, p. 39.

32. Whitehead, *Process and Reality*, p. 39.

33. Plato, *Laches*, trans. Benjamin Jowett, in *Great Books of the Western World*, vol. 7. Chicago: Encyclopedia Britannica, 1952, p. 30.

34. Plato, *Phaedo*, trans. Benjamin Jowett, in *Great Books*, vol. 7, p. 251.

35. Plato, *Seventh Letter*, trans. J. Harward, in *Great Books*, vol. 7, pp. 800–1.

36. Plato, *Republic*, trans. Benjamin Jowett, in *Great Books*, vol. 7, pp. 427–28.

37. Michael Grant, *The Founders of the Western World: A History of Greece and Rome.* New York: Scribner's, 1991, pp. 97–98.

38. Plato, *Critias*, trans. Benjamin Jowett, in *Great Books*, vol. 7, pp. 481, 483.

39. J.V. Luce, *Lost Atlantis: New Light on an Old Legend.* New York: McGraw-Hill, 1969, pp. 176–77.

Chapter 4: Aristotle: How Can Knowledge Be Categorized?

40. Michael Grant, *The Classical Greeks.* New York: Scribner's, 1989, p. 262.

41. A.E. Taylor, *Aristotle*. New York: Dover, 1955, p. 33.

42. Aristotle, *Politics*, in Renford Bambrough, ed., *The Philosophy of Aristotle*. New York: New American Library, 1963, p. 384.

43. Aristotle, *Politics*, p. 383.

44. Aristotle, *Politics*, pp. 388–89.

45. Grant, *Classical Greeks*, p. 261.

46. Aristotle, *On the Heavens*, quoted in Morris R. Cohen and I.E. Drabkin, *A Source Book in Greek Science*. Cambridge: Harvard University Press, 1948, pp. 146–48.

47. Aristotle, *On the Heavens*, p. 148.

48. Aristotle, *History of Animals*, quoted in Cohen and Drabkin, *Source Book*, p. 422.

49. Grant, *Classical Greeks*, p. 262.

Chapter 5: Buddha: Can Suffering Be Overcome?

50. Quoted in Ross, *Three Ways of Asian Wisdom*, p. 80.

51. Quoted in E.J. Thomas, *The Life of Buddha in Legend and History*. London: Kegan Paul, 2003, pp. 31–32.

52. Ross, *Three Ways of Asian Wisdom*, p. 85.

53. Quoted in Thomas, *Life of Buddha*, pp. 50–51.

54. Quoted in Thomas, *Life of Buddha*, p. 65.

55. Quoted in Lin Yutang, ed., *The Wisdom of China and India*. 1942. Reprint, New York: Random House, 1955, p. 360.

56. Quoted in Will Durant, *Our Oriental Heritage*. New York: Simon and Schuster, 1954, p. 427.

57. Quoted in Lin Yutang, *Wisdom of China and India*, p. 361.

58. Quoted in Durant, *Our Oriental Heritage*, p. 430.

59. Durant, *Our Oriental Heritage*, pp. 431, 433–34.

60. Quoted in Thomas, *Life of Buddha*, p. 100.

61. Quoted in Ross, *Three Ways of Asian Wisdom*, p. 82.

Chapter 6: Confucius: How Should People Treat One Another?

62. Confucius, *Analects*, in *The Analects of Confucius*, trans. Arthur Waley. New York: Random House, 1938, p. 91.

63. Lin Yutang, *Wisdom of China and India*, p. 6.

64. Confucius, *Analects*, p. 162.

65. Liu Wu-Chi, *Confucius: His Life and Time*. Westport, CT: Greenwood Press, 1972, p. 176.

66. Lin Yutang, *Wisdom of China and India*, p. 53.

67. Szema Ch'ien, *Shiki*, in Lin Yutang, *Wisdom of China and India*, p. 56.

68. Quoted in Durant, *Our Oriental Heritage*, p. 668. The passage comes from *The Great Learning*, by the ancient Confucian philosopher Chu Hsi.

69. Durant, *Our Oriental Heritage*, pp. 668–69.

70. Quoted in Lin Wu-Chi, *Confucius*, p. 56.

71. Szema Ch'ien, *Shiki*, in Lin Yutang, *Wisdom of China and India*, p. 66.

72. Quoted in Szema Ch'ien, *Shiki*, in Lin Yutang, *Wisdom of China and India*, p. 67.

73. Confucius, *Analects*, pp. 173–74.

74. Quoted in Tomlin, *Eastern Philosophers*, p. 264.

75. Szema Ch'ien, *Shiki*, in Lin Yutang, *Wisdom of China and India*, p. 100.

For Further Reading

Books

Fahmeh Amiri, *The Prince Who Ran Away: The Story of Guatama Buddha*. New York: Knopf, 2001. In this well-written telling of Buddha's life, Amiri uses the surviving ancient accounts and fills in the blanks with snippets of logical guesswork.

Russell Freedman, *Confucius: The Golden Rule*. New York: Arthur A. Levine, 2002. A very well-written and appealing book by an award-winning writer of literature for young people. Freedman makes Confucius and his ideas come alive.

Don Nardo, *Greek and Roman Science*. San Diego: Lucent Books, 1998. This overview of early Western science discusses the era in which science and philosophy had not yet become separate disciplines and provides useful information about some of the ideas and writings of Plato and Aristotle.

———, *The Trial of Socrates*. San Diego: Lucent Books, 1997. Covers the life and ideas of one of the founders of Western philosophy, who exerted a strong influence on Plato and other later thinkers.

Jeremy Weate, *A Young Person's Guide to Philosophy*. London: Dorling Kindersley, 1998. A very ambitious and handsomely mounted book that gives short overviews of important Western thinkers and their principal ideas.

Brian Williams, *Aristotle*. Crystal Lake, IL: Heineman Library, 2002. A commendable general overview of the famous Greek thinker and his writings.

Websites

Aristotle, University of St. Andrews, Scotland (www-gap.dcs. st-and.ac.uk/~history/Mathematicians/Aristotle.html). An excellent brief overview of Aristotle's life and teachings, with links to related topics and information.

Confucius, Stanford Encyclopedia of Philosophy (http://plato. stanford.edu/entries/confucius/#1). This site presents useful information about Confucius's life and ideas and provides links to related sites.

Democritus of Abdera, University of St. Andrews, Scotland (www-gap.dcs.st-and.ac.uk/~history/Mathematicians/ Democritus.html). Another excellent site provided by the University of St. Andrews, this one has a great deal of information about one of the world's first atomists.

Major Works Consulted

Ancient Sources

Aristotle, *Aristotle: Complete Works*. Ed. Jonathan Barnes, various trans. 2 vols. Princeton: Princeton University Press, 1988; also trans. Robert M. Hutchins, in *Great Books of the Western World*, vol. 8 and vol. 9. Chicago: Encyclopedia Britannica, 1952.

————, *The Athenian Constitution, Eudemian Ethics, Virtues and Vices*. Trans. H. Rackham, 1952. Reprint, Cambridge: Harvard University Press, 1996.

————, selected works in Renford Bambrough, ed., *The Philosophy of Aristotle*. New York: New American Library, 1963.

Jonathan Barnes, *Early Greek Philosophy*. New York: Penguin, 1987.

Morris R. Cohen and I.E. Drabkin, *A Source Book in Greek Science*. Cambridge: Harvard University Press, 1948.

Confucius, *Analects*, in *The Analects of Confucius*. Trans. Arthur Waley. New York: Random House, 1938.

————, selected works in Lin Yutang, ed., *The Wisdom of Confucius*. 1938. Reprint, New York: Modern Library, 1994.

Diogenes Laertius, *Lives of Eminent Philosophers*. Trans. R.D. Hicks. 2 vols. Cambridge: Harvard University Press, 1995.

Lin Yutang, ed., *The Wisdom of China and India*. 1942. Reprint, New York: Random House, 1955.

Lucretius, *The Nature of the Universe*. Trans. Ronald Latham. Baltimore: Penguin, 1951.

Plato, *Dialogues*, in *Great Dialogues of Plato*. Trans. W.H.D. Rouse. New York: New American Library, 1956; also trans. Benjamin Jowett in *Great Books of the Western World*, vol. 7. Chicago: Encyclopedia Britannica, 1952.

————, *Plato: Complete Works*. Ed. John M. Cooper. Various trans. Indianapolis: Hackett, 1997.

Philip Wheelwright, ed., *The Presocratics*. New York: Macmillan, 1966.

Modern Sources

H.G. Creel, *Chinese Thought from Confucius to Mao Tse-tung*. 1953. Reprint, Chicago: University of Chicago Press, 1971. One of the better available studies of Chinese thinkers and philosophical schools of thought.

Will Durant, *Our Oriental Heritage*. New York: Simon and Schuster, 1954. Part of Durant's renowned and award-winning series, The Story of Civilization, this massive volume provides detailed coverage of intellectual life in ancient Egypt, Mesopotamia, India, and China, with an especially fulsome and absorbing section on Buddha and his teachings.

————, *The Story of Philosophy*. New York: Simon and Schuster, 1961. A modern classic, this book examines the major thinkers of Western civilization in a concise but thorough manner. Highly recommended.

R.M. Hare, *Plato*. New York: Oxford University Press, 1982. An excellent overview of Plato's life, views, writings, and impact on future generations.

Werner Jaeger, *Aristotle*. Oxford, Eng.: Clarendon Press, 1948. One of the best modern biographies of one of the greatest thinkers of all time.

John M. Koller, *Asian Philosophies*. Englewood Cliffs, NJ: Prentice-Hall: 2002. Koller, a distinguished professor of philosophy at Rensselaer Polytechnic Institute, ably covers the major Eastern philosophical schools, including those of India and China.

Liu Wu-Chi, *Confucius: His Life and Time*. Westport, CT: Greenwood Press, 1972. In this detailed examination of Confucius and his teachings, the author attempts, in his own words, to present the famous Chinese thinker as "a man of flesh and blood," rather than a legendary "saintly figure."

George N. Marshall, *Buddha: The Quest for Serenity*. Boston: Beacon, 1978. A thorough and well-written presentation of Buddha's life and quest for enlightenment.

A.E. Taylor, *Aristotle*. New York: Dover, 1955. One of the best short studies of Aristotle and his thought.

————, *Socrates: The Man and His Thought*. New York: Doubleday, 1952. Another classic by Taylor, this one about the mentor of Plato (who himself mentored Aristotle). Highly recommended.

E.J. Thomas, *The Life of Buddha in Legend and History*. London: Kegan Paul, 2003. An updated reprint of a classic study of Buddha's life, heavily supported by long passages from both ancient and later Buddhist and Hindu writings.

Rex Warner, *The Greek Philosophers*. New York: New American Library, 1958. A renowned scholar/translator here offers a well-written synopsis of the major Greek thinkers, including Democritus, Plato, and Aristotle. Warner provides sample primary source materials for each person covered.

Cyril Bailey, *The Greek Atomists and Epicurus*. New York: Russell and Russell, 1964.

John Bowker, *World Religions*. New York: Dorling Kindersley, 1997.

Edward Conze, *Buddhism: Its Essence and Development*. New York: Harper and Brothers, 1959.

Michael Grant, *The Classical Greeks*. New York: Scribner's, 1989.

——, *The Founders of the Western World: A History of Greece and Rome*. New York: Scribner's, 1991.

Ted Honderich, ed., *The Oxford Companion to Philosophy*. New York: Oxford University Press, 1995.

David C. Lindberg, *The Beginnings of Western Science*. Chicago: University of Chicago Press, 1992.

G.E.R. Lloyd, *Aristotle: The Growth and Structure of His Thought*. New York: Cambridge University Press, 1968.

J.V. Luce, *Lost Atlantis: New Light on an Old Legend*. New York: McGraw-Hill, 1969.

Frank N. Magill, ed., *Masterpieces of World Philosophy*. New York: HarperCollins, 1990.

Nickolas Pappas, *Plato and the Republic*. London: Routledge, 1995.

Colin Ronan, *Lost Discoveries: The Forgotten Science of the Ancient World*. New York: McGraw-Hill, 1973.

Nancy W. Ross, *Three Ways of Asian Wisdom*. New York: Simon and Schuster, 1978.

Bertrand Russell, *A History of Western Philosophy*. New York: Simon and Schuster, 1972.

Chester G. Starr, *A History of the Ancient World*. New York: Oxford University Press, 1991.

E.W.F. Tomlin, *The Oriental Philosophers: An Introduction*. New York: Harper and Row, 1963.

Max Weber, *The Religion of China*. Trans. Hans H. Gerth. Glencoe, IL: Free Press, 1951.

Alfred. North Whitehead, *Process and Reality: An Essay in Cosmology*. Ed. D.R. Griffin and D.W. Sherburne. New York: Free Press, 1978.

INDEX

Abdera, 27, 31, 35, 37
Academy, the
   Aristotle and, 53–54, 56
   Eudoxus and, 60
   Plato and, 43–45, 48
Acropolis, 39
Aegean Sea, 27, 52, 54
Agora, 40
Alexander the Great. *See* Alexander
   III
Alexander III (king of Macedonia),
   56–58, 62
Amyntas II (king of Macedonia), 53
Analects, 76
Anaxagoras, 14, 19–20, 28
Anaximander, 18
Anaximenes, 18–19
animals, 12, 52, 60–62, 74
Ariston, 39
Aristotle
   Alexander III and, 57–58
   animals and, 12, 52, 60–62
   biology and, 60–62
   birth of, 52–53
   categorizing of knowledge and,
     50–52, 58, 61–62
   death of, 62
   education of, 53
   human nature and, 12
   influence of, 12
   on logic, 51, 52
   on theory of
     heavenly spheres, 59–60
     the soul, 33
   Lyceum and, 58
   Macedonia court and, 56
   marriages of, 54
   on number theory, 20–21
   on *physis,* 18
   on slavery, 92
   Socrates and, 17
   writings of, 58–59
   see also animal kingdom; Plato;
     politics
asceticism, 74
Asia, 62, 84

Asia Minor, 18, 31, 54
Assos, 54
astronomy, 46, 60, 62
Athens
   Abdera and, 27
   Aristotle and, 53–54
   Atlantis and, 47–48
   democracy of, 39–40
   Democritus' visit to, 30–31
   Peloponnesian War and, 40
   wealth of, 39–40
   see also Academy, the
Atlantis, 47–48, 49
atomic theory
   atomism and, 21
   atoms and, 11, 27, 29, 74
   death and, 32–33
   Democritus and, 26, 37
   explained, 31–34

Babylon, 30
barbarians, 55–56
Barnes, Jonathan, 17, 34, 89
Bodhi Tree, 71
"Boundless," the, 18, 19
Buddha, 14
   birth of, 67
   childhood of, 67–68
   death of, 75
   Eightfold Path and, 72–73
   enlightenment and, 70–72
   evildoers and, 93
   fabrications of, 67
   Five Moral Rules, 73–74
   the four truths of, 72
   gods and, 64–65
   meditation and, 23, 68, 71
   preaching of, 74
   starvation, self-torture and,
     68–69, 71
   statue of, 65
   suffering and, 23
   as a teacher, 64–65
Buddhism
   religious elements of, 64, 66
   social involvement and, 25

spread of, 12–13, 22–24
Zen, 25

Callippus, 60
Central Harmony (Tsesze), 94
Chalcidic peninsula, 52
Channa, 68
Chao (duke), 84
Charmides, 40
Ch'en, 86
Ch'i, 84, 86
Chin, 86
China, 12, 14
   Buddhism and, 12, 23–24
   Confucius and, 77–78, 86–87
   religious systems of, 24
Chuang-tzu, 14, 24
Chungtu, 84
Cicero, 58
Confucius, 14, 76
   birth of, 79, 81
   Confucianism and, 24–25
   death of, 87
   education of, 81
   exile of, 86–87
   the"golden rule" of, 77, 87,
     94–95
   manuscripts of, 80
   marriage of, 81
   school of, 79, 81
Corinth, 27, 53
cosmology, 32, 38
cosmos, 16, 18, 59, 74
Crete, 48
Critia, 40
Critias (Plato), 47, 48
Crotona, 20

Damasus, 35
Darwin, Charles, 18
David, Jacques-Louis, 42
Demiurge, 44
Democritus, 11, 14, 21
   birth of, 27
   death of, 37
   on early humans, 35–36
   education of, 28–29
   on good government, 89
   influence of, 12
   knowledge of, 26
   theory of the soul and, 33

travels of, 28, 30, 35
treatises of, 35, 38
writings of, 26–27, 37
Dhammapada (unknown), 93
Diodorus Siculus, 35–36
Diogenes Laertius, 26–28, 30–31,
   35, 37
Durant, Will, 74, 82

Early Greek Philosophy (Barnes), 89
Earth
   Aristotle and, 12
   atomic theory and, 32
   Buddha and, 74
   elements of, 59
   spherical shape of, 59
   theory of forms and, 44
Egypt, 28, 43, 47, 48
Eightfold Path, 72–73
"Enlightened One." See Buddha
Epicurus, 21
ether, 59
Euboea, 62
Eudoxus, 60
evolution, theory of, 18

Fangshu, 81
Five Fathers, 81
Five Moral Rules, 73–74
forms, theory of, 44, 50–51, 53

Gae (duke), 87
Galen, 32
Ganges River, 74
Gibraltar, Strait of, 47
Glaucon, 45
gods
   Buddha and, 64–65, 74
   laws and, 15–16
   Mara, 70
goodness
   concept of, 22
   Confucius and, 12, 82
   humans and, 11
   mathematics and, 46
   Plato and, 38
   politics and, 45
Grant, Michael, 46, 50, 63
Great Dialogues of Plato (Plato), 90
Greece
   beginning of philosophy and, 14

Picture Credits

About the Author

Historian and award-winning writer Don Nardo has published numerous volumes about the ancient world, including chronicles of Greek, Roman, Egyptian, and Mesopotamian history; studies of ancient warfare; and biographies of ancient philosophers and scientists. He is also the author of *Egyptian Mythology, Life in Ancient Persia*, and the *Greenhaven Encyclopedia of Greek and Roman Mythology*. Mr. Nardo resides with his wife, Christine, in Massachusetts.